"Feeling old and tired? Caught yourself thinking that everyone from airline pilots to your family doctor are getting younger and younger? Has your sex life been reduced to the late night programs on HBO and Showtime? Or have you reached the top of that career ladder you've been climbing for so long and been wondering of late what its all about? If you answered yes to any or all of these questions then pick up *Playing Life's Second Half.* You'll soon be singing, 'The best is yet to come . . .'"

> —Scott Miller, Ph.D., cofounder of the Institute for
> the Study of Therapeutic Change, and author of
> *The Heart and Soul of Change* and *The Heroic Client*

"David Powell has written an insightful, moving, and practical book that will help all of us who wrestle with the challenges of bringing greater meaning and fulfillment into our lives. This book will change many men's lives."

> —Rabbi Steven Carr Reuben, Ph.D., President, Board
> of Rabbis of Southern California and author,
> *Children of Character: Leading Your Children to
> Ethical Choices in Everyday Life*

D1559843

"'Old age' has taken on a new vitality as baby boomers have learned how to live longer and healthier lives. Instead of sinking into a quiet retirement, many of us are ready to take on new challenges and careers. Traditional male socialization complicates this transition. *Playing Life's Second Half* ... presents a cogent analysis of this process and provides excellent guidance in the construction of a successful road map to life's next horizon."

—Robert Johnson, MD, FAAP, chair of pediatrics and professor of pediatrics and psychiatry, UMDNJ, New Jersey Medical School

"David Powell knows what he's talking about. His own life is marked by stellar achievements in several fields. And yet in his own second half of life, he has shifted from a success to a significance orientation. His book raises the most essential issues for men in midlife and provides practices that guide the reader through his own process of self-assessment and redirection. This book has helped me to treat the men in my life with greater compassion."

—Cynthia Crowner, Executive Director, Kirkridge Retreat and Study Center

PLAYING LIFE'S SECOND HALF

A Man's Guide for Turning Success into Significance

David J. Powell, Ph.D.

New Harbinger Publications, Inc.

Distributed in Canada by Raincoast Books.

Copyright © 2003 by David J. Powell
New Harbinger Publications, Inc.
5674 Shattuck Avenue
Oakland, CA 94609

Cover design by Amy Shoup
Edited by Wendy Millstine
Text design by Tracy Marie Carlson

ISBN 1-57224-335-X Paperback

New Harbinger Publications' Web site address: www.newharbinger.com

05   04   03

10   9   8   7   6   5   4   3   2   1

First printing

To Denny Moon, my dear friend, pastor, and male role model, who has challenged and inspired me all along the way. We have shared similar journeys over many years. Thank you, Denny, for your love and friendship.

Contents

Foreword

The Two Halves of Life: *How* Did We Get Them So Mixed Up?
By Richard Rohr

It is striking how often history has recognized that there are at least two major movements in the spiritual journey. I call them the path of ascent and the path of descent. Jesus speaks clearly to Peter of first "dressing yourself," and when you are older "letting others dress you" (John 21:18). Psychologists speak of having an ego before you let go of your ego. C. G. Jung speaks of the task of the first half of life as being "individuation" and the second half being "transcendence." The wisdom of India tells a man that he is first a student and house-holder, and later a "forest dweller" and a wise man. They all intuited something that we are beginning to see was crucial for cultural survival and personal transformation, and yet modern humanism has largely forgotten it and even denies it. We treat the young as if they were adults, and then we resent the old because they seem so childish. Maybe there is a connection.

I am convinced that untold failure and distortion have entered the worlds of psychological development and transformative spir-ituality because we have not honored these two stages in proper sequence, and therefore have not honored them at all. The tasks, the appropriate energies, and the goals themselves end up being jumbled and confused. When we don't recognize that there are two major life tasks, we usually produce rigid personality structures in the second half of life because they are still idealizing the containment rules for the first half of life. We also produce false surety and grandiosity in young men in the first half of life because they take their petty ego concerns to be final or significant goals. The journey of life's second half seems like pure idiocy to a young careerist who thinks that life is all about upward mobility.

Basically, we have the whole thing backward. We raise children as "liberals" to freely figure out and fend for themselves, and then they rightly seek boundaries, overdo it to contain themselves in midlife, and end up materialists, nationalists, militarists, and power conservatives by the end of life. As educators have been telling us for most of the last century, the natural movement of the developmental psyche is exactly the opposite. We need to begin conservatively, with clear boundaries, identity, a sense of chosenness, and even a kind of specialness and inherent dignity. I like to call it the narcissistic fix that good parents give their children, and good religion gives its adherents. It is surely the best way to start, but it is not a good way to continue and certainly not where the wise man must be and will be at the end of life.

Then, as we grow older in wisdom, age, and grace, we should move toward more compassionate, tolerant, and forgiving worldviews. The dualistic mind breaks down in the presence of divine mystery and human failure. Instead, we largely produce mere ideologues and fundamentalists in the second half of life, who have sadly not done the fundamentals of human and spiritual growth. Or we produce a kind of intellectual withheldness and skepticism that looks like liberal humanism, but is far indeed from any real compassion or generativity toward the world. True holiness and true wisdom are much deeper and broader than mere liberal thinking, however, so do not think I am trying to equate them at all.

Our deconstructed Western culture is so backward that we have actually turned around the classic patterns of human growth. No wonder we have so many suicidal and depressed teenagers, and so many unhappy and bitter old men. We are supposed to move from a healthy conservatism to a healthy liberation from the same, but we start with an utterly false and unwarranted liberalism, and end up with self-addicted and stuck people by the age of fifty. This is not working.

We need instead, as the Dalai Lama says, to "learn the law very well, so we will know how to disobey it properly" (Dalai Lama 1996,

24). From the Bible, Paul makes the same point with different metaphors: "Through the Law I am dead to the Law, so that now I can live for God" (Galatians 2:18). Augustine is even more daring, "Love God, and do what you want!" Such freethinking from the very people that we are supposed to admire shows how unlike them we really are. In fact, such language even sounds dangerous, antinomian, and libertine instead of religious. But that is only to people who have still not completed the tasks of the first half of life! To them it sounds like heresy, and in fact it is—*for them.* But for mature men, who have internalized the values of containment and law, "The human one is master even of the Sabbath" (Luke 6:5).

Until we can again realign society inside of some kind of honest, eldering system, where the elders *do* have something to give the next generation, where they *know* that they have something to give, and where the younger ones are in a position to receive it and appreciate it, I see little hope of understanding the basic teachings of Jesus, Paul, the Buddha, the women mystics, or anyone in higher stages of wisdom. Neither do I see us becoming a mature and healthy culture. We will remain, as Robert Bly says, a "sibling society" where seventeen-year-olds teach seventeen-year-olds nothing worth teaching, where fifteen-year-old children have children whom they cannot mentor, where old men can only affirm one another in their mutual prejudices and fears, and where these very immature and falsely affirmed men then become heads of church and state.

And finally, we will remain incapable of seeing this spiritual immaturity because these heads of state actually reflect the level of moral development of the majority of the populace. Democracy ends up not being much of an asset when it only encourages the blind to elect the blind, and when ambition and wealth control the electoral process. This is not a system that is going to allow the cream to rise to the top. Even Thomas Jefferson said that the success of the democratic experiment depended on certain intelligence among the electors.

When the second half of life is put at the beginning of life, we have old men still asking boyish, egocentric questions about their own significance and superiority because they did not have the containment to test their own mettle and find their inherent value when they were young. We also have young boys speaking with arrogance and a self-assuredness that is totally undeserved. (This has always been true, I am sure, but at least we once had elders who tempered and tested such flights of fancy instead of empowering them.) When the needed clarity of the first half of life is put off until the second, it merely becomes strong opinions, absolutes, jingoism, and cultural imperatives among older men whom we need for integrity, broad-mindedness, statesmanship, and the reign of God. Initiation culturally assured the young man that it was time to put away childish things and to carry an adult persona.

Men still needing and demanding their narcissistic fix lead us too often—old men having erotic dreams of self-aggrandizement, advancement, and ambition; and young men having sterile visions of personal advancement instead of any contribution to the common good. We will be able to believe that a new age has truly come when we see the emergence of true authority and true elders in a society without the father. We will know we are in a new age when we stop needing to hate fathers and mistrust all authority and all masculinities.

David Powell has given his best years to travel the world and introduce twelve-step programs and health care concerns to underdeveloped nations. I thank him for offering himself here as a truly generative, second-half-of-life father and elder. He can talk as he does in this book, not primarily because he has the academic credentials (although he does), but because he has been there and returned with a gift. He has earned the right to speak. He has paid his dues in the first half of life, the dues of acquiring an education, hard work, holding a career and family together, and knowing how to sustain some long-term relationships. He has internalized the values taught therein and then moved beyond them, not protecting his credentials or past relationships but squandering them on risky and new projects. This is mature spiritual energy. This is the Indian forest dweller and holy man. This is the male authority that we need, and it is much more powerful than mere role, title, diploma, or power of office. Things are back in right sequence here, and the wisdom you will find will speak for itself.

—Richard Rohr, OFM
    Center for Action and Contemplation
    Albuquerque, New Mexico

Preface

Baby boomers born before the mid-1950s likely still remember where they were the day John F. Kennedy was shot. Yet, as earthshaking as his assassination was, September 11, 2001, had an even more far-reaching, global impact on the psyche. To write about people in life's second half, I must address the impact of 9/11 on many and how it will shape the way we look at the chronological, social, emotional, and spiritual markers of our lives.

For most, 9/11 brought a time of insecurity and nervousness. After the horror and bewilderment, many sought to find anchors in their lives, to focus on what was in their control, and to let go of what was not. On that day, in a most dramatic way, we saw how little control we had over our lives. Husbands, fathers, sons, wives, mothers, and daughters went to work that morning, as every other day, and never returned home and were wrenched from their families.

Perhaps the central lesson of 9/11 is the need to find a sense of one's inner self. The success symbolized by the World Trade Center and the Pentagon and the power, possessions, and prestige embodied in those buildings could be destroyed in seconds. So too can the treasures we build up and hold onto in our lives be quickly snatched from us. What remains is the significance of our lives, loves, and light that lives on in others.

This book invites you to find a sense of your inner self, your significance, that will outlive any successes you have achieved thus far in life.

Acknowledgments

This book is about men and hopefully will be read by women as well. For everything I have learned from the men in my life, I acknowledge their impact on this book: the men at the Center for Action and Contemplation's Men's Rites of Passage; the men interviewed for the book; male friends and colleagues I've known over the years. I honor a few special men who have played key roles in shaping this book: Archie Brodsky, my editor and friend; Richard Rohr and Jerry May, my spiritual mentors; Milton Powell, my father, who took the time to play baseball with me and, in so doing, taught me about fatherhood. To Stan Obitz, who, in college, introduced me to new worlds of thought. To Spencer Smith, my editor at New Harbinger Publications, who guided me through the book's writing. To Bob Fuller, my longest-term friend. And to so many other men, who I hope will forgive me for not naming them all.

And a special thanks to the three women in my life who have shared my journey and passions and supported me all along the way: Barbara, my wife and friend, who has loved and supported all of my crazy dreams and to whom the chapter on relationships is dedicated. I also thank Heather and Kiersten, my two lovely daughters, who have been the delight of my life.

—Thanks to all.

Introduction

Every seven seconds, another America man turns fifty. The baby boomers, the largest age cohort in world history, are becoming "senior boomers." In the next ten to twenty years, as the boomers enter the second half of life, America will move from being a youth-oriented culture to a senior-oriented culture. This demographic shift combined with other changes, such as medical and public health advances that open up the possibility of a longer active life, are arguably some of the most significant changes in the history of the United States. Despite the importance of these demographic changes, in general, American men are ill-prepared for what lies ahead.

As record numbers of men enter the second half of their lives, they face fundamental questions about what it means to be an aging man in our culture. The journey in life's second half is not about success as measured by power, possessions, and prestige. Although some men may still be struggling with economic and social issues, the second half of life should be about *why* to live, and not just *how*. Central to life now is the inward journey instead of the ascent upward. The second half of life means moving from the question "What do you want to do?" to "What do you love? Where is your passion? What gives you meaning and purpose, a sense of significance in your life?"

When do you enter the second half of life? Is it when you turn a certain chronological age, such as fifty? Is it when you go through a proverbial "midlife crisis," accompanied by a career change and a new red sports car? Is it when you face the inevitable physical changes and you are not able to do what you once could do? It may arrive when you encounter a broken marriage or a shortened career. For many, it is the realization that you have more than you ever wanted, yet still ask, "Is that all there is?" Whenever you cross over into the second half, the journey is quite different from the first half.

Digging Deeper: Moving from Success to Significance

The theme of this book is that the second-half journey requires you to dig deeper to find new sources of refreshment, as your central motivating force moves from achieving success to finding significance. Success is usually measured by something or someone other than yourself. It has an external locus to it. Significance, on the other hand, has the quality of something from the inside out, a mark made inside of you which then makes a mark on the world.

Thus, the theme of this book is moving away from an external locus of control, by which you followed someone else's plan for your life (your parents, your employer, your family) to finding your destiny. What is it you were created to be? What do you wish to leave as your heritage in the lives of others? The way you do that is the spiritual journey of digging to find your roots, the ground of your being, and finding new sources of meaning in your later life. It necessitates coming to terms with existential issues such as death, the meaning of work in your life, retirement, and your relationships with friends, women, other men, your children, and your father. Much of the second half is living in between endings and beginnings. In fact, living in the difficult times, in the paradox and mysteries of life, is an essential task of the second half. Finally, the second-half journey will bring you to wisdom, from aging to "saging," to being a wise man (Schacter-Shalomi and Miller 1995).

Five key spiritual principles recur throughout the text. How you live out these basic spiritual principles is the essence of the second-half journey.

- Life is difficult.

- You are not in control.

- You are going to die.

- You are not all that important in the grand scheme of things.

- Your life is not about you. There is a far bigger story being written.

These principles are the cornerstone of this book, which will show how to find meaning in life's second half if you embrace them. You need to throw away the old, tattered, and currently unhelpful maps you used in the first half of your life. The book will help you create a useful road map to guide you along the path of life, with all of its important side trips that you must take if you are to age well.

How to Use This Book

This book is for men who are either in the second half of life or looking ahead to what it might be like when they get there. Although written about men, it is not exclusively for them. On the contrary, it is meant to be accessible and helpful for women who seek to better understand the men in their lives. It is for all who want to find significance in the second half, to find a spiritual path that provides meaning and purpose.

This is a self-help book, which means that you are in for a lot of introspection, reflection, and activities to assist you in this journey. The second-half journey is a complex trip, requiring continuous searching and disciplined practices to find meaning. This book is a guide that requires your active engagement. Simply reading through the issues may be interesting, but little will change for you unless you seriously consider and apply yourself to the questions and recommended exercises. You can begin the task of finding meaning for the second half of your life by taking an inventory of yourself. Change will occur when you answer questions, do the exercises, try the techniques, and practice the skills offered. But change is not simply a mental or even behavioral process. It requires a shift in attitude in the foundation of your life. Ultimately this is a spiritual book, encouraging you to explore your spirit and the basic questions about your life and your connection to something greater than yourself.

It is recommended that you keep a journal when reading this book. You will be instructed at various points to take out your journal and answer the questions posed. Keeping a journal (paper or computer-aided) enables you to apply the book to your specific journey in life. Buy a good journal. Put it on your desk or near your easy chair. Today and every day you read a section of the book, allow yourself time for reflection and writing in your journal.

Everyone is unique. The book can only provide you with a basic road map. You need to adapt and apply these materials to your unique self. Instead of thinking about men and their fathers in the abstract, you should explore your relationship with your father. Instead of absorbing abstractions about work and retirement, you will learn about your work and what you want to be in the second half. Digging deeper is an active process. No one but you can dig deeply into your own life. And the time to start examining your journey so far and what lies ahead is now, regardless of your age. Over time you will observe changes, albeit subtle, in your life. You will find a pattern or path emerging. Seeing change will be enormously reinforcing as you face other profound changes in your life.

The recommended journey in this book will pay off as you find new ways of looking at your life and its meaning. This book should provide you with the following benefits:

1. It offers a new vision of the male journey in the first and second halves of life.

2. It provides tools for dealing with midlife changes.

3. It assists you in moving from success, the driving force for most men in the first half, to significance, the essential journey in the second half of life.

4. It enables you to reflect on key relationships in your life, such as you and your father, you and your children, and you and your partner.

5. It assists you in learning how to play again or perhaps for the first time, how to laugh at yourself, and how to relax and contemplate the important issues in life.

6. It offers you a chance to ask anew the ultimate questions of life, "How am I significant?" and "What gives me meaning and purpose?"

7. It helps you redefine retirement and feel a sense of purpose after your work life.

8. It provides tools to help you face your eventual death and the death of others.

9. It provides a road map for endings, life's in-between times, and new beginnings.

10. It focuses on where to find new sources of spiritual refreshment in life.

11. It provides the tools for you to move from aging to saging, to being a wise man.

My Story

An essential part of becoming wise is being the keeper of the story, the bearer of meaning. By listening to others' stories and by telling your own, you will find yourself engaged in something greater than yourself. As the first of this book's vignettes about men in the second half of their lives, I will tell you my story.

As I write this book, I am fifty-eight, clearly in life's second half. I have worked in the health care field for thirty-eight years as a marriage and family therapist and substance abuse counselor. I worked for twenty-five years as a businessman, struggling with the pressures of managing a growing business. For years I sought through the business to implement my clinical goals and ethical values in behavioral health care. I retired in 1999 from my position as president of the company, which I founded in 1974. So my professional life has included business, health care, and psychotherapy, synthesized, to a degree, in the company I managed for years.

At this point in my life I am busier than ever, speaking, writing, and offering simple services to others. What I do today is both different from and continuous with the first half. Although I am doing different things, some activities look much like what I did before. But what I now do is with a different spirit. That is the essential shift for me in the second half, choosing to do things because of their significance, not because they will bring success. If success comes, it is a wonderful but secondary gain.

For example, the current love of my life, after my family, is assisting the Chinese government in establishing twelve-step programs such as Alcoholics Anonymous in China and training Chinese health care professionals to treat substance abusers. Although in the first half of my life I also sought to help others through my practice and my corporation, now it is no longer about me, my prestige, my power, or my popularity. It is about a legacy that will be left behind in the lives of others.

My current passion is an outgrowth of my previous work. But the spirit of what I am doing is quite different. How you remold the materials of life's first half to the second is what gives the second-half activities significance and creates a different experience out of them—rather than simply going off and doing something different. Buddhists say what you are today is a reflection of what you were and what you will be is found in what you are now. Finding the connections between the first and second halves of your life is this book's essential journey.

My spiritual journey is the center of my life. I am a spiritual man. I have studied theology and hold three master's degrees in divinity. I practice qigong (an ancient form of meditation in motion) and I have studied with teachers such as Thich Naht Hahn, the Vietnamese Buddhist master. Yet, my spiritual journey continues to be an adventure filled with surprise, wonder, awe, and sometimes more questions than I have answers. Huston Smith, the philosopher of religion, uses the analogy of a basketball player with one foot firmly rooted, as his pivot foot, while the other foot can move around, exploring different angles and sides to the issues. My pivot foot is firmly rooted in my Christian religious tradition. My other foot is able to explore issues and questions as seen through the eyes of other traditions. I believe this is the essence of the spiritual journey in the second half of life—exploring questions from different viewpoints while remaining rooted in your history and traditions, living with unanswerable questions, and being comfortable in that in-between place. Often the questions are more revealing than finding the answers. This does not mean that I do not hold to certain truths; it means that I am constantly learning, exploring, and seeking a deeper understanding of truth.

As you read this book I encourage you to engage in these questions, seeking wisdom and not knowledge, insight and not data, and learning to live with the questions as much as the answers.

Chapter 1

Bones, Groans, and Hormones: The Male Journey

Our house sits on the side of a hill. In the fall the hills are covered with red-, orange-, and amber-colored oak and maple trees, with the falling leaves an omen of the rigors of the winter that lie ahead. Our house is the first house you encounter as you drive up the hill. The disadvantage of this location is that cars speed by as they accelerate down the hill, heading for the main road. The advantage has to do with water. The development uses a private water company drawing from a well at the top of the hill. By the time the water runs down the hill, the water pressure is strong. We never have to worry about an adequate water supply. Unfortunately, another disadvantage is that the private water company charges captive customers whatever it wishes.

Several years ago, some outraged customers were tired of the endless annual rate hikes. We had two choices. One was to give up ever taking a shower again, an option that had limited appeal to most of us. For our two teenage daughters, not being able to wash their hair for twenty minutes a day was not a pleasant thought. The second option was for each household to dig their own well in their yard. It would provide us individually with an endless supply of low-cost water. Yes, we might lose some of our treasured water pressure, but it seemed a far more attractive option than daughters with dirty hair.

So we explored the possibilities of digging a well in our backyard. Now this area of New England is built on solid rock. Each spring the bowels of the earth spit up rock that has been under the surface for eons and tosses it so it pierces each area of the yard, especially the vegetable garden. To burrow down and find water in the rock proved a costly option as we explored it with well diggers.

So too it is for men in the second half of life. A tug says you need to find new water, either because the old water supply has become too costly or because the well has run dry. Finding new sources of meaning and nourishment can be a painstaking but necessary process. As a young man you might have thought of seeding the clouds to make rain more abundant. In your youth the sky seemed unlimited in what was available to you. But in the second half you need to explore downward and inward to another source of water, one that flows from within life itself. The journey no longer is upward to new heights. Besides, you likely do not have the same energy to be the youthful rainmaker and to progress professionally and personally to new heights. And even if you do have that energy, it is at a dear price physically, socially, emotionally, and spiritually.

There are men who ascend throughout their life, men who society admires in their later years as well as in their youth. We hold up examples such as Yeats, who wrote his best poems later in life, or Hitchcock, who made powerful films in his late fifties. Saul Bellow wrote well into his eighties, and Jacques Barzun was prolific in his nineties. Thomas Mann wrote *Doctor Faustus* and *Confessions of Felix Krull: Confidence Man* after age seventy. Picasso was producing masterpieces into his nineties. Architect Frank Lloyd Wright began his most creative work at sixty-nine. Other men who blossomed in their later years were musicians Vladimir Horowitz, Arthur Rubinstein, and Pablo Casals. Verdi composed *Otello* at age seventy-three and *Falstaff* when he approached eighty. In jazz and theater we have Benny Carter, Doc Cheatham, Eubie Blake, and the Broadway centenarian George Abbott. Philosopher Alfred North Whitehead published his most influential works after sixty-five. In the media there is Daniel Schorr, now in his eighties, who enjoys a second career as an author and a National Public Radio commentator, whose clarity of voice sounds like a younger man.

Playing life's second half is not about how productive you are in your later years. Rather, it is what drives your effort and the spiritual changes that create a different vision of yourself. Although we cannot know for certain, what likely brought these men greatness later in life was a new source of nourishment, rooted in a deeper understanding and awareness of life, welling up from within them. Some may have risen to greatness later in life simply by already being big celebrities. Some perhaps because they continued to develop their lifelong discipline. Some may have declined in their technical abilities as a result of aging but excelled through deeper understanding as they aged. We do not know for certain. But as demonstrated by these men, the aim of life's second half can be to plant new roots that grow and nurture a rich form of life, filled with fulfillment and meaning beyond power, possessions, prestige, and privileges. This may necessitate being guided by someone who will say to you, "Dig here to find the water of life." That is what this book is about: where and how to find new water for your soul in the second half.

This book is about the journey to streams of living water, the journey from places of dryness and wilderness to life, vitality, love, acceptance, and gratitude. The primary thesis of this book draws on the work of Father Richard Rohr, a Franciscan priest from New Mexico, George Vaillant, and other authors, as well as my own life experiences and interviews with hundreds of men over the years.

In the end, we never dug a well in the backyard, but physically, emotionally, socially, and spiritually I found a new source of water and refreshment in my life.

Crossing Over: Biological, Social, Emotional, and Spiritual Markers

When do you cross over into the second half? Everyone crosses over differently, marked by biological, social, emotional, and spiritual changes. These markers represent guideposts in the male journey of life, signaling life transitions.

Chronological and Biological Markers

The changes that happen to your body in midlife may have indicated that you crossed over into the second half. Anybody who says he can still do at fifty what he was doing at twenty wasn't doing much at twenty. Aging brings limitations in what you can still do. But biology does not program a series of events to mark the beginning of middle adulthood the way puberty announced the onset of adolescence. Your body has been aging since your early twenties but so imperceptibly that it took decades for these changes to become apparent. Holding a book farther from your eyes may keep you from noticing that your lenses are stiffening, but one day, usually in your forties, the arms become too short and reading glasses become necessary. As difficult as it is to accept changes in vision, men strongly deny any decline in hearing. Having glasses is far more acceptable than needing a hearing aid.

Here are the inescapable facts about aging: We age at different rates. Even within one person, organs show different rates of change. However, some generalizations can be made based on data from the Baltimore Longitudinal Study of Aging begun in 1958 (Vaillant 2002, 81). Remember though, these statements do not apply to all people.

Heart: It grows larger with age. Maximal oxygen consumption during exercise declines in men by about 10 percent with each decade of adult life. However, cardiac output stays nearly the same as the heart pumps more efficiently.

Circulation: For some, the heart slows down and is less able to pump blood through the body, resulting in less energy and stamina for physical labor. Decreased circulation makes people over fifty more sensitive to cold, especially in the hands and feet.

Lungs: Maximum breathing capacity may decline by about 40 percent between ages twenty and seventy.

Brain: With age, the brain loses some cells and others become damaged. The brain adapts by increasing the number of connections between cells and by regrowing the branchlike extensions that carry messages in the brain.

Kidneys: They gradually become less efficient at extracting wastes from the blood. Bladder capacity declines.

Body fat: With age the body redistributes fat from just under the skin to deeper parts of the body. Men are more likely to store it in the abdominal area.

Muscles: Without exercise, muscle mass declines 23 percent for men between ages twenty and seventy. Exercise can prevent this loss.

Sight: Difficulty focusing close up may begin in the forties. From age fifty on, there is increased susceptibility to glare, greater difficulty seeing at low levels of light, and more difficulty detecting moving objects.

Hearing: It becomes more difficult to hear higher frequencies with age. Hearing declines more quickly in men than in women.

Taste: The sense of taste diminishes at about fifty, resulting in fewer taste buds. Sweet and salty tastes seem to be the first affected.

Bones: Bones become weaker in men in their sixties.

You can either view these facts as decline and become depressed, or you can adapt to changes in your body and see the positives of increased creativity, improved coping skills, the ability to take more responsibility for your health, and greater self-confidence. Other positive changes in aging include a greater capacity to love, a deeper sense of gratitude, and an expanded sense of play and humor. The question is, will you bemoan your bones, groans, and hormones, or celebrate your creativity and ability to love?

It is important that you accept that you are in the second half and not to try to act as if the sweet bud of youth remains. Perhaps this scenario is familiar. You play basketball with teenage boys at a picnic. Even if you beat the teenagers, the physical pain is hardly lessened by the thrill of victory. Tom Seaver, the New York Mets pitcher, at forty said, "I throw as hard as I used to. It just doesn't get there as fast." Satchel Paige, the baseball pitcher who played well beyond the age of most ball players, asked, "How old would you be if you did not know how old you wuz?"

Using a simple chronological marker for when you enter the second half fails to account for biological variations among men. Data showing progressive changes in body functions have to be taken with caution because they refer to average changes. Hidden in the averages are people with silent, undiagnosed diseases and men who smoke and drink to excess, eat unwisely, and lead sedentary lives. A purely chronological marker of aging is inadequate, for it fails to account for the myriad variables affecting aging and biology.

Nearly 70 percent of older men say that their health is excellent, very good, or good. Even with chronic illnesses, most men feel they are "doing okay physically" (Vaillant 2002, 12). In no other season of life is the range of physical responses so varied as midlife and beyond. These changes have forced us to study aging from a new perspective. The biological markers alone do not determine how old "old" is.

We need images of the second half that are free from traditional chronological confines. Some people figuratively die at fifty but are not literally buried until they are eighty. As the longevity game continues to be played, fifty is what forty used to be. You may need to adjust the lens of what midlife looks like as the median age of men increases. If it simply adds biological time to your life, not matched by an expansion of awareness, your life can be depressing. Thus, we must also look at social, emotional, and spiritual markers, wherein you begin to learn that fulfillment in life is not a result of tacking on points to a single scoreboard. Perhaps the second half is when you see the power of the mind and spirit, rooted in your experience, and emotional maturity, grounded in rich, social relationships.

Answer these questions in your journal:

☒ What physical changes have you noticed in recent years?

☒ What physical limitations do you have that you didn't have ten years ago?

☒ What are you doing to delay these changes? To face them?

Social Markers

For men who have children, somewhere between the time your children became teens and when they left the house, you entered an empty-nest lifestyle. But even this traditional marker is changing as men in their forties and fifties are becoming fathers of young children. Matt was forty-four with a seven-year-old son. He said, "I went to my twenty-fifth high school reunion and all the men said they were fathers of young children. One of my classmates came in with a pregnant wife. We were so relieved that we were not the only late bloomers. Someone else was even later in starting a family than us." It makes little sense to mark the beginning of midlife with the departure of children from home, given today's variations in child-bearing age and child-rearing patterns.

Other social markers may be when you started doing different things. For example, it might be buying a red convertible sports car or telling your spouse you want to quit your job of twenty-five years. You may go through a marathon-man phase where, at forty, you pump iron or train for your first marathon. Career changes have always been a social marker. But that too is undergoing change. It is estimated that baby boomers will average ten jobs in their lifetime and at least three major career changes. Nearly one-third of American men in their forties have changed not just their job but their occupation. So changing jobs or careers may say less today about a man than traditionally.

Another social marker is the "midlife crisis" that typically happens somewhere in your forties or fifties. It can be a time of disruption and fear that life is slipping through your fingers. You may question your values, marriage, job options, beliefs, and purpose. Even if you were fortunate to enact your earlier vision—write a successful novel, reach the top of the corporate ladder, have a sound marriage and family—you may find that fulfillment did not bring the happiness that was supposed to come with success. Achieving that dream may have cost you too much. If you attained only part of what you dreamed of, you might see that partial success as a failure. You may find yourself modifying an earlier dream, downscaling it to a manageable size and reducing its power over your life. You may recover a dream put on hold at the beginning of adulthood. You may take your reworked dreams and continue advancing, seeking to ascend within the structure you had before, still building on youthful images. Or you may abandon your dreams, bow your head, and accept defeat.

Max went through what his family called a midlife crisis when, at age fifty, he quit his twenty-year job as a salesman to open a retail auto parts store. "I have always been fascinated by cars. I wanted to have my own business. Sure, it was financially risky, but it was something I had to do to find out if I could run a business. Although it brought great distress to my family, I needed to pursue it," Max said. "I had to find out if I had it in me."

Not everyone goes through these changes and they are not as tumultuous for all as they may appear. In fact there may not be a universal crisis for men. Troubling events may spread out randomly over the years. But clearly, by midlife there is generally an accumulation of social events—chance encounters, tragic losses, shifts of fortune, changes in relationships, job changes, and so on—which add up to the reality that the second half will be different from the first half.

Respond to these questions and instructions in your journal:

☒ List the changes in your social life in the past ten years. What things do you do today that you did not do ten years ago?

☒ Which of your dreams from the past have you reworked?

Emotional Markers

Four issues affect the emotional markers of the second half. The first is how you feel about aging. It's said, "You're only as old as you feel," which does not seem to help much on the days when you feel like you are old. Perhaps you crossed over into the second half on those days when you said, "I don't have the same passion about life as I did before."

Phil, fifty-six, said, "I have a nice house, a big mortgage, a good job, and kids I'm proud of. I have more than I ever dreamt I'd have. I have things I have locked up in my garage but nothing in my heart. I'm chasing after something that I don't care about anymore." Tony, fifty-eight, for thirty years has struggled as a freelance artist. He has had some success yet never made a great deal of money. Now, as he faces the future without a pension plan or safety net under him, he asks, "Do I still keep trying to make it big as an artist? Can I be satisfied with the modest success I have achieved? What will the future look like for me without financial security?"

Second, how have you dealt with your power so far? Perhaps you crossed over into the second half when you realized there are things in life you cannot control. Joe said, "I lost my salesman job after fifteen years with the company. I always thought I'd retire there. Everything was under my control, or so I thought. Now, what do I really want to invest my life in? What do I really care about? How do I construct a life that fits the me of today as opposed to what I was? When did I lose control of my life?"

Along with confronting your loss of control often comes a loss of hope. "Why try?" Peter said, after being downsized out of a job he held for thirteen years. But remember, the loss of control is not the end of life but life's beginning. There is good life after you face your powerlessness.

Third, how have you handled your emotions and how strong are your support systems? Contented, calm, easygoing people tend to age as "happy-well" versus "sad-sick" people. Also, the lack of emotional support systems exerts a powerful effect on health. The death rate climbs steadily as relationships dwindle, with rates running from two to four times as high among the totally isolated as among those who are married, have extended ties with family and friends, and are active in social groups offering emotional support. In your youth you reveled in a sense of individuation, autonomy, and independence. In the second half you seek connectedness, relationships that bring a sense of interdependence.

Fourth, the second-half viewfinder is clouded by the way your culture looks at aging. Ram Dass (2000) visited a friend in India, who greeted him with the words, "You're looking so old! Your hair is gray." Ram Dass reacted with a typical Westerner's horror. Calling someone old in America is a bad label. In other countries, being old is an achievement that entitles you to respect and recognition. In some countries people cherish wrinkles, look forward to their first gray hairs, and exaggerate their age to gain respect. But most Americans fear aging and do not harvest the emotional fruit of a lifetime's experience.

Answer these questions in your journal:

☒ How old do you feel?

☒ What things do you see as outside your control?

☒ How strong are your emotional support systems (family, friends, work associates, community)?

☒ What does your culture say about getting older?

Spiritual Markers

The second half is a spiritual journey that seeks a new source of meaning. "Spiritual" is a perplexing word, conjuring up images of church, synagogue, mosque, temple, and religion. For me, spirituality is the hatching of the heart, an unfolding from within. It involves the discovery of your inner, sacred self and the connection to that force which impels your life. It involves your core identity, your sense of awe, and your commitment to your value system. Spirituality honors a presence of something greater than you.

All of us have a longing to be spiritual, to invest our energy in things that matter, and to find significance in what we do in everyday life. No one can make you spiritual, for you already are a spiritual being. Philosopher Pierre Teilhard de Chardin (1968) wrote that we are not human beings having a spiritual experience but spiritual beings having a human experience.

Up until midlife, society taught you how to live. Spirituality tells you why to live and what to love. It is the opening of your ordinary life to something greater than yourself, a purpose and value system that transcends your everyday life. It involves finding the sacred in your ordinary life. At the heart of the journey is a look inward to what you truly love and want, a journey to find significance.

Spiritual wisdom is different from intellectual knowing. By midlife your memory is turning on you. Your life is no longer dedicated to demonstrable, provable bits of facts. Now the emphasis you put in your life is more about what you truly love. The names of the last five presidents of the United States may be less important to you but the birthdays of your grandchildren are more important.

No longer does the test consist of true-false questions but rather multiple-choice questions that may not have any correct answers. Sitting with an unanswered question may be more helpful than finding an answer. As you age you come to see that life's problems are not to be solved but lived in. In your youth you wanted someone or something to tell you what to do, what the answers to life are, to help you to know the blueprint for salvation. As I embrace life's second half, I am not interested in that stance any longer. These questions bore me. I'd rather explore the images and questions and live into the mystery of life.

To live into the mysteries, the spiritual journey calls you to listen to the still, small voice within and a quiet mind free from the baggage of distorted desires. In Taoism, the questions are, Do you have the patience to wait till your mud settles and the water is clear? Can you remain unmoving till the right action arises by itself? To have this sense of presence you need stillness to find your center. Rainer Maria Rilke writes in *A Book of Hours*, "And in the silent, sometimes hardly moving times, when something is coming near, I want to be with those who know secret things or else alone" (1996, 59).

Also, you need to enjoy the journey and not be too intent upon arriving anywhere. You need to act from the heart and love with compassion. This requires you to offer humble and simple service. A spiritual maxim for the second half is, Until the water clears serve others. Stay tuned to the world around you and allow your wounds to be mended by being in contact with others' wounds. Gautama Buddha directed us to not close our eyes before suffering. Instead, we are to find ways to be with those who are suffering by all means, and to awaken to the reality of suffering in the world. Jesus said, "If you have done it to the least of these you have done it to me" (Matthew 25:40). The spiritual journey means being where the suffering is, knowing its quality, and holding its babies in your arms.

Mark, forty-six, had a successful practice as a therapist, treating middle-class people for middle-class problems. But he still felt unsatisfied and wanted to have a more direct impact on people. So he sold his practice and joined the Heifer Project, which provides livestock for poor families worldwide to support themselves and produce their own food. He did not close his eyes to the suffering of others. For the first time in his life he felt truly alive.

The fruit of the journey is shown in how you live. Some men become statements of peace, learning to live more lovingly, to resolve conflicts without aggression. Some look at racism and find ways to end it. Some work to reduce the consumption of mass-produced items that exploits cheap third-world labor. Some help build houses for organizations like Habitat for Humanity. Some coach teams, mentoring young boys in the technique of playing baseball and in what it means to be a man of honor. Some learn to recycle, drive less, eat locally produced food, plant trees, and begin to live in a way that respects others. Others live simply so others can simply live.

Finally, the spiritual journey requires role models who can point out the road ahead. Baby boomers have age scouts, people sent ahead to check out aging and tell us it is okay to be fifty or sixty years old. They dust off the future so when you get there it will be cool to be sixty. Boomer age scouts are people like Paul McCartney,

Paul Newman, Gloria Steinem, Ringo Starr, and Paul Simon, none of whom were boomers, but all turned sixty and are still rocking and rolling. Chuck Berry is the first seventy-year-old rock icon. These age scouts reflect what life might be like in the future for us. Most have done so by facing adversity in their lives—Ringo's recovery from addictions and Paul McCartney's loss of his wife, Linda, John Lennon, and George Harrison point the way to changes ahead for us.

The danger with age scouts is that they become heroic figures like in your youth: "See how successful I can still be, like them." To make these age scouts heroes is to continue the first-half journey of ascent. We focus on the public persona and not the personal pain each age scout has experienced. A better image than these public icons are the figures who may not have achieved notoriety or fame but left an indelible mark on you. They are your spiritual mentors who fit comfortably into the background, offering wisdom when asked, providing new ways of living and working together, offering gentle images of mortality. They teach you about artistry, fruitfulness, birth, and death. They remind you of discipline while focusing on harvest time, healing, wholeness, and fruition.

Paul, sixty, had a career as a salesman for a company. In his fifties, after his recovery from alcoholism, he began a not-for-profit organization dedicated to interfaith religious dialogue. He became a model of service and peacemaking for younger men.

The chronological, social, emotional, and spiritual markers are best seen from the overall perspective of the male journey through life, indicating where you have been, where you are now, and what might lie ahead for you. Life is understood backward but lived forward. You live life as if you were looking in the rearview mirror, better able to see where you have been than where you are going. A road map of the journey can help in understanding what you can see in the rearview mirror and what might lie ahead for you.

The Male Journey

Before you begin this section, in your journal write five statements that begin with the phrase, "Today, I am _____."
Did you describe what you do or what you are? Did you speak about your role as worker, father, husband? These are descriptive of what you do. "I am" statements speak to what you are feeling today, who you are, your inner self, your hopes, dreams, fears, and aspirations. You spent the first half describing yourself as a human doer. The second-half question is about becoming a human being, who you are.

The Journey of Ascent

Did you hear these messages when you were young? "Grow up. Become a man. Become independent. Climb the ladder of success. Be all that you can be. You can do anything you want to do. You can be anything you want to be." If so, you began on a typical male journey through life with these messages to ascend. This is the heroic journey with idealistic visions and encouragement from family to experience your own power and possibilities. With this came a natural sense of necessary egocentrism. For many families the son was the center of attention. To be a man meant

- To be responsible for your family, the watchman of the gate, the breadwinner, the strong one, the protector. Duty was important.

- To be a hard worker. If you worked hard enough, you would succeed financially, socially, professionally, in relationships, and so forth.

- To delay gratification. If you worked hard, your rewards would eventually come. Religion told you there would be pie in the sky when we die by and by.

- To accept a black-and-white world where truth would always win.

- To be competitive. "Winning isn't everything. It's the only thing."

In the first half you ascended the ladder and were told to love your work, family, career, and success, to devote your energy to proving yourself. It is fitting that the Army uses the slogan "Be all you can be" to recruit young men because in the first half that has meaning. But in the second half that slogan may mean that a man might leave routine work behind in order to discover and express the depths of meaning and passion in his being, whether through more satisfying work or other spiritual or personal activity. Youth is a time of degrees and accomplishments as we are schooled in attainment and achievement. The second half is a time of meaning and articulating different aspirations.

Although the push for competitive achievement also exists for girls growing up, this is a very different message from that traditionally given to young women, such as my wife, Barbara. Growing up in Kansas, she was taught that she had three career choices: a teacher, a secretary, or a nurse. Of course these careers would be only temporary, until she undertook her true calling, to be a mother.

As a young man, perhaps you headed to college to find a career. Maybe you were drafted into the military during the Vietnam years and fought for a patriotic cause. Perhaps you went into a trade. Or you might have taken the countercultural route in the 1960s and become antiestablishment, opposed to the things we were taught to value: success, power, possessions, and prestige. But then the 1980s came along. It became cool to win, to have possessions. What changed? We did. After a flirtation with a simpler life, we bought into the American ideal of being "thing-focused" men.

Male Initiation

Traditionally, boys were initiated into manhood in their teen years. Initiation involved a vision quest that had boys experience their own limitations. The boy was told, "You are not in control. There are forces greater than you. Being a man means to live with pain and a sense of your limits." Typically this male initiation occurred in nature where the boy experienced a sense of awe and wonder. There is a primal calling into the wild where nature teaches the boy about mystery and insignificance. To understand this principle you need only to sit in the midst of a storm or be afloat in a boat on the ocean. This sense of vulnerability accompanied by a wounding was part of the initiation.

However, in the past two centuries male initiation declined in most Western societies. The boy never hears these messages and is told only about the journey of ascent. Young men today (especially in poor nations and urban ghettos) drop out, knowing they will never have power, prestige, and possessions. They become angry young men, without a sense of purpose, ambition, or commitment to anything other than survival.

The contemporary experience of gangs, gender confusion, homophobia, aimless violence in schools, and the romanticizing of war has replaced traditional male initiation. The boy lives in the realm of being rational, a problem solver, without any confrontation of his spirit. He comes to believe in the philosophy of progress, autonomy, and development of the individual. He misses the lessons of old that life is more about surrendering than concluding, trusting than fixing, gratuitous grace than glory. Today, without leaving the Garden of Eden, the boy (or man), when faced with the world of contradictions, is overcome with the burden of being a man.

Thus, boys growing up today seek to climb the ladder of success. Many achieve the American dream of all the prizes that go along with success. Given this focus on ascending the ladder, is it any wonder that men die an average of seven years younger than women? Men have heart disease at twice the rate of women, ulcers twice as often, and suicide rates six times higher than women; they work in more dangerous jobs and are far more likely to hurt themselves and others through alcoholism, drugs, violence, and abuse of their body. Men are four times more likely to be murdered than women. This is the price men pay for the journey of ascent without initiation into manhood.

The Midlife Crisis of Limitations

Somewhere in the middle of life, typically in your forties or fifties, you face a crisis of limitations and identity. You climbed the ladder of success only to see that the ladder was against the wrong building. So you have all these toys and still you ask, "Is that all there is?" Jerry says, "Now that I have all these things, I still am unhappy. I don't know what I love anymore. I do not have a sense of meaning and purpose in my life. I provided for my family, did all the right things. So what! Is that what it means to be a man?"

Midlife crisis is sometimes accompanied by a sense of loss and failure. By midlife you likely have experienced some form of pain: loss of a loved one, a broken marriage, career changes, job loss through downsizing, addiction, death of a parent or the premature death of a friend, or physical limitations. Joe says, "I had it all until my son got very sick and died. There was nothing in the world that could take away the pain of that loss. For the first time in my life I had to face that my life was out of my control." Midlife brings us face-to-face with massive change. It is a journey of transformation, a crisis of limitations, the realization that you cannot have it all. Midlife brings you to questions such as "Who am I? What is life about?"

You may act out this pain by trying to regain your power and control at work and over the family, or pushing yourself physically to show you can still do it. But the heroic virtues of the first half do not work anymore. The paradox is that when you are confronted with your limits, then and only then can you find the mysteries of life. At this proverbial fork in the road you find honesty and humility by letting go of your effort of self-control.

When this happens, midlife becomes a summons to grow anew, a challenge to change, a beckoning inward to a new wholeness, a turning point to your true self. You have spent life's first half trying to live out other people's dreams of what you should be, seeking success in those dreams. You are now crossing from one identity to another. The reality of the second half is you have entered a mystery that you will never fully understand. Carl Jung said at the end of his life, "I do not know the meaning of life. It remains an unsolved mystery to me" (Jung, Jung, and Wolff 1982, 114).

The Three Roads Ahead

There are three roads you can take at this fork. The first road is that you still try to ascend the ladder even higher. If you have not ascended the ladder to the heights you thought you should, the pressure to ascend in the second half can become even stronger, to make up for lost time. Society has icons of second-half success, men who continue to gain more power, prestige, possessions, and privilege. In so doing they also become one-dimensional, shallow men who continue to be driven by materialism and outward appearance. At some point they likely find they have it all, yet are left with nothing.

Harry, fifty-five, owns two highly profitable real estate companies, lives in a townhouse in New York City, and hobnobs with all the sophisticates in the city. He is a millionaire several times over. But he feels he doesn't have enough. He lives for gaining greater wealth. When his daughter was married, Harry was barely involved in the wedding. Although he did find the time in his busy schedule to attend the wedding, it was a nonevent for him because he operates on only one dimension, power and possessions. The highlight of the wedding for Harry was that his daughter was marrying a wealthy man.

The second path is taken by most men. We do not age well. Check it out. Go to a retirement home and see the angry, embittered old men, hollow shells of what they once were, without joy or meaning in life. Or talk to men in their fifties or sixties and ask them what they look forward to after they stop working. Many will say, "I will continue to work forever. After all, what else would I do? Without work I am nothing."

Men who take the rusted-out journey never come to terms with their pain. A concept repeated throughout this book is if you don't transform your pain you transmit it. And men on the embittered journey have never turned their wounds into sacred scars. They continue to look for someone to blame. They remain negative, critical, and unhappy men. Addictions to sex, alcohol, sports on TV, toys, and work may be all that gives them meaning. They may remain physically active in their later years, but what they did for a living defined them. When they no longer work or when work rejects them through downsizing, they become angry, dispassionate, and burned-out.

There is a third way, the journey inward to new sources of life. This is the wisdom journey, becoming a wise man. This way usually involves a spiritual guide. It does not come naturally for it runs contrary to the cultural messages of ascent. Deepening, going inward, shows that the old rules no longer work. You need to stop trying to ascend the ladder. Success has little to teach you after forty.

The deepening journey involves surrender, letting go of control, abandoning competition, power, possessions, and prestige. It involves finding compassion in life. It often requires some painful insights, what St. John of the Cross (1995) called "the dark night of the soul." It involves time in the wilderness, as Moses experienced for forty years, Jesus during his temptation, the Buddha when he sat at a tree waiting for enlightenment, and Muhammad when he listened for God's revelation. This requires embracing your shadow, which you resisted facing all your life. Mythologist Joseph Campbell (1988) speaks of this journey as an initiation into the dark of the unconscious, a call to adventure, in which you withdraw from the external to the internal world. It involves going through a dark place and finally emerging into light.

Essential to this journey is to move to a larger, spiritual sphere that embraces others and their story. In the first half you focused mostly on "Your Story," as puny, boring, and insignificant as it may have been. Your story is subjective, personal, and psychological, and is the subject matter of far-too-many TV and radio shows and New Age articles. It is too small a story. Somewhere in the first half you also focused on "Our Story"—our traditions, where we live, our family, our group, our community, our country, and even our religion. As important as that is, there is a greater story that unfolds, which we can call "The Story." In "The Story" you realize you play a small but vital role in something greater than yourself, a cosmic story found in a sense of interdependence with others, your world, the Earth, the universe.

Answer these questions in your journal:

☒ Have you ever felt a call to go deeper in your life? If so, how and when did this happen? Where has it led you? What have you learned?

☒ What is changing for you on your inner journey to your true self?

☒ What's been your experience of darkness? Have you experienced a significant time of darkness in your life? How has darkness been a teacher for you?

The Last Stage of Life

Let's move beyond the road map to what I see as the last stage of the journey. After you go inward to new sources of passion, you can turn outward in an expression of that transformation. In the deepening process you contemplate yourself, a stage that may last years. But if you stay there, you have only gone halfway through the process. You need to allow that new light to shine through you into the lives of others. No more need you be concerned about what others think of you. You can spontaneously respond to what others need. No longer driven by first-half ego needs, you can live a life of joy. This journey is through the crisis of limitations, the false self, to the true self, to new joy. Emerging is a man of greatness. Power comes not from without but as a result of the inward journey to find your true self.

A Vision of the Third Way: The Journey to Your True Self

What might the second-half journey be for you? The Buddha said the best predictor of what you will be is what you are today. Research has shown us the best predictors of aging well. According to the Harvard Adult Study (Vaillant 2002, 203–11), there are several key dimensions you need to cultivate to age well, most of which involve the downward and inward journey of deepening:

- A sense of generativity, investing yourself in something that will outlive you

- A sense of tolerance, patience, open-mindedness, understanding, and compassion

- Maintaining health by abstaining from smoking and alcohol abuse, maintaining a healthy weight, a stable marriage, and exercise, and having adaptive coping skills

- A sense of joy in life

- A sense of subjective life satisfaction not found in outside measurements

Instead of viewing the second half as a time of decline you need a vision of life as a time to discover inner richness and transformation. Out of inner growth comes saging, becoming a wise man, where healers and role models for future generations are born (Schacter-Shalomi and Miller 1995). Becoming a wise man does not automatically happen just by living a certain length of time. You become wise through inner work that leads to expanded consciousness.

Charley is eighty-five, with an amazing sense of joy. It seemed to blossom even more after the death of his wife. Some day I want to be a little like Charley in his contentment with life. Arnold, at eighty-two, had a career as a psychiatrist, served his country in the Korean War and the early years of the Vietnam War, and speaks with great authority and wisdom. He does not speak much, but when he does you listen. At the core of his being is a connection to his universe that is evident in what he does. Paul is eighty and deeply involved in dialogue with people of various faith traditions. Through his leadership, his organization sponsors conferences that attract hundreds seeking to better understand and appreciate different faith traditions. These men, although not famous, are men of greatness, for they have followed the deepening path to find their true self.

The journey to the true self can be illustrated by imagining the layers of an onion. You must go through a journey that peels back the layers that have accumulated over time. Your false self defined you to the outside but was really not what you were created to be. The outer layer is what people see of you, what you want them to see. The false self may also be a compliant front, formed over years of doing what others wanted of you, with or without tangible external rewards or recognition. What lies beneath is what is hidden from others, your sexual life, your view of romance, your relationships. If you go deeper within yourself, you face your addiction to sex, work, money, alcohol, drugs, or gambling. The false self, though, is an illusion. It does not really exist. It is not really you. It is only what you pretend to be.

If you dig deeper you come to a black hole, your shadow, the hidden part of you that you never want to face. To get through this black hole you must go through a wilderness of loss. Finally, after that journey, you come to your true self, that which God or something greater than yourself created you to be. Your true self is a reflection of that image. When you find your true self, you find your true significance.

In this journey you find the well that runs deeper. You find a new love, not necessarily in human form. It is what theologian Paul Tillich (1951) called "the ground of your being" and mystic Meister Eckhardt in the fourteenth century called the origin and the ground (1996).

Exercise: Your False and True Self

Answer the following questions in your journal:

1. What hold do power, possessions, and prestige still have on your life?

2. How does your false self impact on your attitudes about life?

3. To what are you addicted?

4. Rank the periods of your life from most to least satisfying (ages 1–9, 10–17, 18–22, 23–29, 30–39, 40–49, 50–59, 60–69, over 70). Which period was most satisfying? Second most satisfying? Third?

5. What were the most important milestones in each decade?

6. How would you describe your first-half journey? A journey of ascent?

7. What were the costs of the ascent journey?

Exercise: A Timeline of Your Life

- On a piece of paper, draw the timeline of your life. What have been the significant events in your life so far? The milestones? The turning points?

- Write your memories of your first day of school, first love, first kiss, first illness, high school and college milestones, significant achievements, failures, career changes, marriage(s), divorce(s), children.

Conclusion

Whether you have followed the traditional journey of ascent or another path, playing life's second half means to face the essential question of how to turn success into significance. We will now explore the road map of life's second half, and I will offer a guide to move from success to significance.

Chapter 2

September of Your Years: Midlife and Beyond

Midlife is a time to face your limitations, to reflect on your significance, to approach the summit of your work life, and to move through the crossroads between life's first and second halves. As noted in the preceding chapter, you are faced with several important choices at midlife that may determine where you spend the rest of your life.

Your Significance at Midlife

Tom was in his mid-fifties and dying of cancer. As he lay in his hospital bed, by his side were his wife and children. In a fading voice Tom said, "I never did enough." Mary, his wife, said, "Don't ever say that. You were a good husband and provider." "Yes," Tom said, "but I never did enough." Tom's tearful adult daughter said, "Dad, don't say that! You were a wonderful father, always there for me. I love you, Dad." Tom said, "Yes, but I never did enough." His son said, "Dad, you have been a great father. I looked up to you. You taught me so much." "Yes, but I never did enough. I did not take enough time off." They all insisted, "You were more than we could ever ask for, you were more than enough." Tom said one last time, "No, I meant I did not do enough *for me*."

Midlife is a time to reflect on what you have done for yourself so far in life. Midlife is also a time when you may feel a blankness, sameness, aloneness, that comes from your questioning what all of your "doings" and accomplishments were about. "So what?" you ask. "Amidst all I have done in life, what have I really done?" Yet, you are more than your accomplishments. You are the sum of what you have loved and lived. What is remembered from your life is alive in the hearts and minds of others.

Exercise: Describing Your Significance

1. Make a list of your accomplishments so far in life. From this list, what will people remember you for?

2. Now, write about what you have loved in life: people, your home, your family, work, a redeemed social condition, the experience of making music or playing a sport, or the smiles in the faces of children you met.

3. Rewrite what you just wrote about yourself in light of what you truly would like said about you. What now is important for others to know about you?

Midlife: Somewhere between the First and Second Half

To fully understand what midlife and beyond is about, we must return to the differences between the first and second halves of life, as shown in this table.

Table 1: Life's Two Halves

First Half of Life	Second Half of Life
Achievements, gains	Integration, losses
Doing	Being
Outward and upward progress	Inward peace
Either-or thinking	Both-and thinking
Right and Wrong	Living in between
Finding answers	Sitting with the questions
Self-centeredness	Sensitivity to others
Living out of your false self	Living with your true self
Knowledge, information	Wisdom
Success	Significance

Somewhere between the first and second half comes midlife. Actually, midlife is a doorway through which you pass between the two phases of life. It happens as a result of the erosion of the biological, social, emotional, and spiritual forces converging on you in life's first half. These forces usually are couched in outer life events. Almost any event or combination of events can be the catalyst for opening the midlife doorway to the second half. You do not choose the midlife experience any more than the twenty-month-old child chooses to join the ranks of the terrible twos. A new stage of change chooses you. A call to the inner life becomes real. Midlife begins.

What Is This Thing Called "Midlife Crisis"?

Midlife is more than a crisis. It is a dialogue with your most profound questions about why you live: "Is this the person I want to be in the future?" It is a summons to change, a turning point, a time when you can no longer live by the dreams and habits of your youth. It is a gradual unfolding, a chance to turn to greater wholeness. It is a journey to a new, unknown, and uncharted destination, a time to be less concerned with being lost and more about waiting to be found, a time of profound and meaningful exploration—if you allow it to be so. For meaning does not come to you in finished form, ready-made. It must be found, created, received, constructed. You grow into it.

Midlife also means resurrecting an unlived life. In adulthood you sacrificed many parts of yourself on the altar of success, responsibility, and the expectations of others. To support yourself and your family, to achieve financial and social standing in the community, you likely stifled and censored the voices of your authentic self. So you wake up one day and no longer know what that self is. With the dawning of the second half, voices clamor for expression in the world. Those voices are like a child pulling at you, saying, "Hey, you promised to play with me and never kept your word."

Exercise: Your Midlife Years

In your journal, answer the following questions:

1. Ask yourself what years you would define as your midlife years (ages 35–40, 40–45, 45–50, 50–55, etc.). What changes have you noticed in your midlife years? Describe these changes. How do you feel about these changes?

2. About how much of the time do you feel bored? Do struggles that formerly claimed much of your emotional life seem to have subsided now?

3. If you feel you cannot make a major change in your career, what best describes your reasons why?

4. Did you have a mentor, an older, nonparental person who helped guide, encourage, and inspire you? Do you have one now?

5. What is important to you today? (For example, autonomy, achievement, romance, family, financial security, fame, recognition, meaning, intimacy, spirituality, creativity.)

6. Thinking about your stage of life, how secure do you feel about being able to change positively in each of the following areas: finances, career advancement, spiritual strength, sexual prowess, power or status, mental alertness, memory, serenity, physical attractiveness.

7. How do you typically react to rough spots, problems, or crises in your life? For example, do you work more, become

creative, develop physical symptoms, drink more alcohol, use drugs, seek sex, pretend there is no problem, talk to someone, wait out the problem, or carry on normal activities?

8. Since you turned forty, are you less or more competitive; interested in close relationships; able to manage life's issues; interested in sexuality; accepting of others; spiritually involved?

Midlife as Spiritual Change

Midlife is fundamentally a spiritual reorientation, a shift of focus, a new way of being in the world. As you enter your second-half journey you begin a period of a second naivete, a new middlescence, a second childhood in which you become both like a child all over again and begin anew the process of creating, paradoxically growing into a new, more mature phase of life. This change may come slowly, but often it comes in giant leaps of faith.

Midlife spiritual change involves the following principles:

- Dying always precedes new life, birth, and transformation. New life comes from decay, from what is undesirable. Sickness, suffering, dying, and even death itself are redemptive. Everything can be put to use in the process of growth.

- Waiting is part of moving from one stage to another. This means living in the wilderness times of life, as we shall see in a later chapter.

- You must be willing to enter into both the giving and receiving of great love. Your transformation and liberation are a call to set others free.

Midlife's Central Spiritual Themes

The central themes running through most midlife journeys are

- Ongoing struggles and inner battles, anxiety about essential questions of life, a search for meaning, where there are no maps or directions.

- Fear of the unknown in what lies ahead. A sense of loneliness and not belonging, a longing and restlessness. Periods of confusion, inner dying, disillusionment, disappointments, lost dreams, and reevaluation of your life.

- A gnawing sense of your mortality. Facing the loss of loved ones and your own and others' illnesses. Grieving over the loss of relationships and the accompanying emotions of sadness, anger, self-pity, and depression.

- A sense of failure, even though you may be very successful. A sense of your limitations and the recognition of your shadow. The push to still be productive and a struggle with your competitive urges and success orientation.

- A stronger sense of connection to others, compassion, a desire to use your abilities in a lasting way, generativity (passing on to others the talents you have learned over the years). Periods of clarity and insight, a greater sense of meaning, direction, and purpose.

- A movement to interiority, a focus on the inner world, your creative side. A time of healing or longing to be whole and recovery from old wounds.

- A desire for union with something greater than yourself, such as God and nature and an acceptance of the mysteries of life. A growing need for relationship, rootedness, commitment. Balancing your needs for extroversion and introversion.

The following steps can assist in moving through these midlife spiritual passages.

Step 1: Go Inward

Seek your true self by checking the path on which you have been traveling. Listen to your heart; seek meaning in what you do by exploring spiritual questions. Ask lots of questions, knowing there are likely no answers to these questions. Be open to and aware of what is so. Look at the choices open to you and take risks. Find something about which you can be passionate. Accept life's ambiguities and learn to let them be.

Step 2: Seek Solitude

Find time alone to let your heart rest from the busyness of each day. Spend time being quiet, listening to your inner voice. Cut back on activities and consider downshifting at work. Practice prayer or meditation.

Step 3: Find Others

Strengthen your support systems by joining a spiritual growth group, or a group of people who share common, healthy values. Do not go through midlife alone but find companions and a wise, spiritual friend. Reach out for help and understanding. Cherish your friends; honor your wise elders.

Step 4: Seek Forgiveness

Face your fears by being patient and know that whatever may trouble you today, it too shall pass. Trust the process, as painful as it might be at times. Forgive yourself for your past, your failures, and your disappointments. Let go of your expectations.

Step 5: Seek Wellness

Be good to your body by exercising, staying healthy, and eating well. Slow down and learn to play and laugh. Try to have one good, hearty laugh before 10:00 A.M. each day. Don't take yourself and life too seriously. Relate to children in a new way. Watch the thousand serendipities that are sent your way each day, be surprised, and feel blessed.

Midlife: A Time of Healing

Healing is essential in midlife. All of us need healing for the wounds that bind us, that we carry from the first to the second half, the pain we have not transformed but still transmit on to others and ourselves. You are healed by your wounds. Healing happens when you see that you are lovable just as you are.

Also, although midlife may be characterized by aloneness and loneliness, these emotions need not kill you. Time heals wounds. What you see as your failures are really your teachers. Healing happens when you know that the loving part of you can always out-wrestle the hating part of you. Ultimately, you come to see that your struggle to find a spirituality that enlivens your life is less difficult and complex than you think.

Now answer these questions in your journal:

☒ Visit a wound of your past that you consider to be healed. How was this wound your teacher? What wisdom did you receive from this woundedness?

☒ What or who has been your source of resiliency during the time of healing?

☒ Choose one of your wounds. Ask yourself, if someone were sitting in a chair across from you and experienced this same wounding, what approach to healing would you take with that person?

Midlife Hope

Hope is essential to making the transition from the first to the second half, through the no-man's-land of midlife. Midlife can be a time when, as Thomas Kelly says, there is a "cosmic mother tenderly caring for all" (1992, 27). This is a rekindling of hope as you find that failed hope does not prove the failure of hope. Also remember that hope that goes unlived remains an empty hope. The dreams, hopes, and longings that go unlived in midlife will likely never be lived.

Exercise: Finding Your Hopes and Dreams

Respond to these exercises in your journal:

☒ Write a dialogue with one thing that you hope for in the future, a dream you have long held for your life.

☒ If you wrote a song for your midlife, what would be the lyrics, the music?

☒ Describe a time in your life when you were most hopeful.

Exercise: Visualize Remembering and Letting Go

Step 1

Picture yourself in a forest where it is green and alive with the sounds of birds, the wind in the trees. There is the sound of a stream that flows beside the path on which you are walking. It is warm, with the smell of flowers in bloom. You lie down at the edge of the stream and place your arms in the water. It feels very soothing and comfortable as the bubbling water washes over you.

Someone who has offered you comfort in your life (such as a friend, a parent, a partner) comes and sits beside you. The person is there to give you strength, comfort, and support. You feel the warmth of their caring for you. The person promises to be with you.

Step 2

Now remember a wounding that happened to you earlier in life, when you were hurt, disappointed, or abused verbally or physically, when some negative messages got into your head that influenced you as an adult. Feel the comfort of the person beside you, and the help they offer. With the help of your friend, send this wound downstream, let the water wash it away. See it flow along, out into the stream, dissolving in the great waters of the ocean.

Step 3

Remember a hope of yours that has gone away, a dream you held onto in your heart but seems to be far away from you now. Recall what chased this dream away (fear, busyness, doubt, others' opinions). Feel the love of the person beside you. Now send whatever keeps you from living your hopes and dreams into the water. See it flow along, down the stream, into the faraway ocean. Imagine that hindrance dissolving in the great waters.

Step 4

Remember someone you once loved who no longer is in your life. The relationship seems like it cannot be recovered or mended. Note your feelings about this person. Sense the deep compassion of the loved one beside you. Gather together your lingering feelings and let them drift away with the tears, into the stream, dissolved in the great waters.

Step 5

Lie there in the grass for a while longer; hear the quietness of the woods and water about you. Then slowly move away and hear the soft whisper of the person who lay beside you moving away, knowing they will return whenever needed. Arise from the stream, touch the water one last time, receive the joy given to you, and leave the water, slowly returning to this time and place.

Exercise: Reflecting on Your Journey

Step 1

Write your key assumptions about life that formed the foundation for your attitudes and behaviors before you entered midlife. Look at these assumptions from your midlife perspective. Which ones have you discarded? Which ones have you rearranged or adjusted? Now reflect on the new beliefs and assumptions that are developing or have begun to take root in your life at midlife. In what ways are you seeking deeper meaning?

Step 2

Now try something new. Go for a slow walk in the park, or stroll leisurely on a busy street or on the beach. It doesn't matter where. Let yourself meander aimlessly for awhile. This is an excellent example of what midlife and beyond is about: the journey to an unknown or uncertain location, without a path, and even without a goal. The second half is about the living, not the getting there. It is a letting go of expectations. And if you are patient, you will find a way to do that without letting go of hope.

Conclusion

A Yogi Berra saying is "When you come to a fork in the road, take it." The second half of life is one fork after another. At midlife, will you take the road leading along the path of continued ascent or will you turn inward to find new sources of purpose and meaning in your life? The road that you take will determine where your joy and satisfaction will be as you play life's second half.

Chapter 3

Success and Significance

As we have seen, the journey of life's second half is about moving from success to significance. Success has little to teach you after forty, whereas finding purpose in living is the fundamental task in the second half and has everything to teach you. The key questions after forty are "Where is your passion? Where do you matter? How do you make a difference?"

What Success Means to Men

As we explored in chapter 2, in our culture, men are seen as success objects. Unlike women, who have been assigned benefits based on appearance (and treated as sex objects), men believe they must achieve success. Affluence, prosperity, and power—the rewards of success—encourage men to seek a lifestyle characterized by the cars we drive, the size of our homes, and the straightness of our children's teeth. Because most aspects of a man's life in the first half are evaluated on performance criteria, men dread the possibility that they won't perform sufficiently well. The worst five-letter word to describe a man is "loser." This emphasis on success in life's first half predisposes us to compete with each other. We believe we will be loved and accepted only if we are winners.

In the film *The Great Santini*, Robert Duvall plays a father who cannot drop the competition even when he plays basketball with his son. He plays so hard that he is willing to hurt his son if that is the cost of winning. He will even deny a loss to maintain his ego. Success, to the father, is everything.

Women, on the other hand, do not seem to have this same scripting as they grow up. I recall my daughter in elementary school. The kids would line up to go through an obstacle course. The girls hung at the back of the line while the boys pushed and shoved to be first. I said to Heather, "Go to the front of the line. You'll get more turns that way." She preferred to stay back with the other girls and talk. "Where did she learn that?" I asked my wife. Apparently Heather learned at an early age that competition and performance were not all that important. Relationships seemed far more essential to her.

In the summer of your life, the need to be successful drove you to place value on symbols such as titles and corner offices. It may have caused you to feel excessively pleased when someone important recognized you and to feel hurt when someone passed you on the street without saying hello. The need to know that you are important motivated you in your youth to become an outstanding electrician, researcher, plumber, musician, whatever, to spend hours looking through a microscope, practicing scales, growing a business in hopes of making a fortune. It caused people to try to add to the store of beauty in the world by finding just the right color, the right word, and the right note. And it led ordinary people to buy six copies of the local paper because it had their name or picture in it.

Recognition, though, can be found when you integrate a sense of significance into work, perhaps shifting the emphasis from success to significance within the same activity, or not feeling a conflict between seeking success and significance. For example, the radio recently told the story of a tugboat captain in Maine who rescued Navy men from a sinking ship in World War II. Now, at ninety-three, he is still a tugboat captain and a great raconteur. This is clearly someone whose life's work is in harmony with, and an expression of, his spirit. No big change in recognition is needed in his life.

On the other hand, many men find themselves in settings that proclaim their insignificance. Therefore, you may do desperate things to reassure yourself that you matter to the world. Mitch said, "Can you believe it? At forty, I changed jobs to one I hated, only because I thought it would finally bring me recognition. I despised every day at work. Although I made more money than before, I felt empty. I left the job at fifty and realized I did not matter at all in that job. They found a replacement for me in a week. What a waste, spending ten years of my life chasing after recognition."

Financial success is how we can reassure ourselves that we are important. We rarely speak about how much money we earn. That final frontier is what we use to measure ourselves against others: "How large is my bank account?" Instead, we use the symbols of success and prosperity to communicate our worth. We use our busyness to show how important we are. We have cell phones, pagers, beepers, e-mail, and answering machines to demonstrate that we are so valuable that people need to reach us at any time of the day and anywhere in the world.

However, we confuse notoriety with celebrity and celebrity with importance. Our value cannot be measured by our busyness or our bank account. Significance runs from deeper sources than success.

Answer these questions in your journal:

☒ What did success mean to you in life's first half? What does it now mean?

☒ In what ways are you competitive? What have you done to get notoriety?

☒ Analogous to women being like sex objects, in what ways do you feel like a success object?

Exercise: Men and Money

To determine the role of money in your life, take this self-assessment:

1. Describe your current attitude about money. How important is it to you? Do you derive security from it? Do you use it to measure your self-worth? Your success? Do you feel that you have enough money and assets? If not, how much more do you think you would need to feel comfortable, secure, and successful?

2. What would it mean to you to lose your life savings? To be poor?

3. What is your practice with money? Saving? Spending? Self-indulgence? What do you need to change about your current practice with money?

4. List your material possessions: cars, houses, toys, computers, clothing, and so forth. How important are they to you? What if they were destroyed in a fire?

5. How do you believe your attitude toward possessions affects your spiritual life? Do you believe these attitudes enhance or detract from your spiritual life?

6. How do you need to change your current practice and attitude about possessions for a happier, healthier life?

What Does It Mean to Be Significant?

Fall and winter reveal things summer conceals. As I look out my office window, the leaves of summer have fallen from the trees, and I can see much deeper into the forest in our backyard. My vision seems more clear, although less sunny. Paths that were clogged in summer with vines and branches now open up and I can walk in places not possible in other seasons. I now can see the inner life of the woods behind my house. They seem to have awakened with the clearing away of the summer clutter of nature. Beneath the shell of the bud is sap in gestation that awaits in the barrenness of the fall woods. The colors of spring tinge the nudity of winter. In winter there is a new beauty you see, one refined by experience.

Graciousness is another aspect of this beauty. Much like nature in autumn, aging is a time of spacious love and compassion, of an attitude of goodwill and thoughtfulness toward others. It brings the capacity to affirm life in the face of losses. It is courage grown larger in the face of disillusionment. Much like the woods behind my house, inviting me into spaces I could not go in summer, aging also brings a new sense of beauty and grace. The woods invite us to break from the natural boundaries that confined us in the summer.

James, age seventy-two, says, "Something wonderful happened at sixty. I became aware of the beauty of New England autumns in a way I never had before. When my best friend from college died at fifty-nine, I had to reassess the life I created. The pressures I worked under no longer seemed necessary. Making more money was meaningless to me. If I were not acceptable as I was at sixty, I never would be acceptable. So I simplified my life and downsized my living, and something amazing happened. I came alive again. I had new energy and vigor. Every moment became precious to me in a way I had never experienced before. It is too bad my best friend had to die for me to learn that lesson."

Answer these questions in your journal:

☒ In what ways do you yearn to matter somewhere? Can you accept that you matter not because of your achievements but because you are loved? You are a beloved son.

☒ Where are you going to find significance and who will go with you?

☒ What is it about significance that you fear? Do you fear giving up the journey of ascent to success, fearing you will not be important? FEAR is often *False Evidence Appearing Real*, based in the past and triggered in the future. Your invented fears about being unimportant serve a purpose: they give an excuse to change by degrees. If you put away your false fears, you may learn to choose passion instead of power and significance instead of success.

The True Meaning of Significance

The key to finding significance in life's second half is allowing your roots to grow deeply into the soil of your life to find the taproot. In nature, the taproot is a large single root that finds nourishment as it grows downward in the soil. The plant above ground seeks moisture from its taproot. Like plants, in life you need to dig deeper to find the taproot of your life where true significance is found.

When growing downward, you also may face less light as the shadows deepen. However, photographically, the afternoon is the most interesting time of day. Colors become more vivid instead of being baked in the light of full sun. Subtleties abound as well, such as our awareness of the afternoon hues and evening sunsets.

According to the *Dictionary of Word Origins* (Ayto 1990, 509), the root word for success means "to get next to them," "to follow them." It connotes "doing well, prospering, following under someone else's wishes or direction." In life's first half, you likely spent considerable energy following someone else's wishes for you and meeting the financial, social, and emotional needs of others.

Exercise: Significance and Success on the Internet

Step 1

Try this experiment. Go to the Internet and look up the word "success" through your favorite search engine. In my search on the Web, I found millions of references using the word "success." Almost all of the Web sites to which I was directed discussed how to dress for success, interviewing skills to get a high-paying job, or finding a career for success. My favorite site was about becoming a millionaire in three years. Most focus on wealth building, time management (so you can have more time for wealth building), and spending all the money you will make from being successful.

Step 2

Now search the Internet for references on the word "significance." My Web search on the word "significance" was far more limited, one-fifth as many references as "success." There were very few references having to do with wealth. The focus was almost exclusively on finding purpose in life, statistical significance in mathematics, or questions of value. Does that tell us anything about our materialistic society and what appeals to us?

Significance is what holds something together. The physicist Niels Bohr states that without significance we have incoherence; whatever is assessed becomes "a thing." "All of the toys I have accumulated in life mean very little to me now that my son is ill," says Brett, age fifty-one. "What is the value of stockpiling wealth when the most important part of life, my family, loses their health? Who can put a price tag on that?"

Let us more clearly understand the difference between being successful and being significant. The former has the quality of external measurement, following under or after someone else. Success is to play out someone else's game, seeking the power, possessions, prestige, and positioning that the world tells you are necessary to be important. This is a first half of life goal, driven by the need for success. Significance has the quality of expressing something from the inside out. To be significant is to have a mark made already inside of you that in turn makes a mark on others. You are significant when you write something inherent to you in someone else's life. Significance is to play out your meaning and destiny in life.

Significance Begins in Integrity

"I want to count somewhere," said Mitch, a fifty-year-old corporate executive. "The handwriting is on the wall: I cannot base my life's worth much longer on the power I hold in the company or even at home. My kids merely tolerate my advice. If I want to count, it appears I will need to exercise my voice more subtly, through influence."

Finding significance involves answering these questions: "What will my life add up to? Do I want to be remembered as the man I have been up to now?" This search is one of seeking integrity, balance, and authenticity. Integrity involves integrating the serial identities that have served you through your first half, shedding outlived roles, letting go of the "big shot" ego, and honoring your better nature. It means forgiving your parents and yourself for what had to be, and arriving at coalescence, where you see that all things belong and blend into a whole. You are who you are. This is true significance.

If you study the great spiritual teachers throughout history, you find that as they aged there was always a tendency to find integration, synergy, a bringing together of polar opposites into one being. Everything belongs in the end. Can you say that about your life? Can you live with the tension of opposites while finding ways for things to belong?

Steps to Finding Significance

Finding significance is all about finding ways in which you make a difference, not as you did in life's first half but in the small ways in which you impact on someone else's life. True significance always begins in love, in giving and receiving it from others. Most of the following steps toward significance involve some form of loving yourself and others.

Step 1: If you are still trying to show off for people, forget it! You'll never feel significant, for there will always be someone bigger and stronger, with more money and power than you. Take your eyes off of others. Stop envying what others seem to have, for it will only frustrate you. Can you accept today the riches you have, however small they may seem to you? The reality is that you have everything you need to live, for you are what you are, and that is enough.

Step 2: Realize there is a difference between what you want and what you need. You likely have all you really need by now. You have enough suits, ties, shoes, toys, and material possessions to last a lifetime. One more shirt will not add one ounce of happiness to your life. It will only make you endlessly crave another. Give up your struggle and craving for things. It is the root of your unhappiness in life. Enjoy what you have. Love your children no matter how they turned out, love the beat-up old car you drive, love the partner who sleeps beside you at night, who makes strange noises while she sleeps; love everything in your life!

Step 3: Embrace getting older. You will age no matter how you look at it. Get over it! Let go your envy of the young. It will do nothing for you. Accept who you are by finding out what is good at each age.

Looking back only makes you competitive, and aging is not a competitive sport.

Step 4: Try this experiment. Much as divorce does not seem real until the final divorce papers arrive, write a letter to yourself stating that as of today you are divorcing yourself from the consumerism that has driven you in life's first half. Money is not a substitute for tenderness. Finding love is the only road to significance. Write about what materialism has not given you and the parts of you that you sacrificed in your journey of ascent. Now read over your letter and file it away. Whenever you are tempted to get back on the climb of ascent up the ladder of success, reread your letter.

Significance is found in offering others what you already have, not just in material things but in terms of your experience, wisdom, and love. For example, as I write this book, my mother is ninety-two and my father is eighty-eight, both in good health. As they clean out their house to simplify and downsize their life, I have little interest in their material goods: the silver service, the cut glass, or their furniture. What I am interested in receiving from them some day are those things that have defined them, made them who they are, the things I love and treasure about them. I'd love to inherit my father's tattered Bible with his endless notes in the margins, written over seventy years of study and reading. I want a few strands of my mother's tatting (the lost art of lacemaking) that her fingers have produced for as long as I can remember. This is what makes them significant to me, not their house or their material goods. Heather, my daughter, asked to have the Christmas tree ornaments and decorations she remembered being under the tree every year, handmade buildings and figures made by her grandparents that she fondly remembers from her childhood with them. These are the things that define Grandma and Grandpa to her.

Answer these questions in your journal:

☒ What are those objects that others find significant about you? What are the things that you might leave to your grandchildren or friends?

☒ What traits or emotions do others find to be significant in you? Is it your compassion, your capacity for laughter, your playfulness, your love? Is it your commitment to improving others' lives and making a better world?

☒ How can you live with more integrity than you have previously shown with your family, your community, your employer, and your world?

☒ In what ways can you make the world a place where others can feel joy?

☒ In what ways can you honor others more than you have thus far? How can you show your love to others? How can you promote others' talents and contributions?

Conclusion

May you work less and play more. Earn less, spend less, parent more, stay married longer, live longer, and be safer to be around. May you have dear friends and be closer to those friends than before. May you take a long-term interest in the earth and its gifts and have outdoor pursuits of a quieter and more experiential kind. May you enjoy sexuality more, be more alive in your body; may you be more confident, less needy, less in a hurry. May you be a father who is involved, positive, and willing to take a stand, without being intimidating or confining. May you inspire others to act. May you learn to play more music, appreciating all that you hear. May the cult of youth disappear for you, so that you don't envy young people but are available for them to seek the wisdom you possess. May you be a role model to others in a warm, unhurried way, yet still passionate and humorous about all you do. May you be revitalized spiritually and religiously. May you decide what you want from work rather than have work decide for you. May you spend some time every year alone, in solitude—when possible, in nature. May you work for organizational and societal change where it is needed, always seeking peace and justice in the world and in your corner of it.

Chapter 4

The Men and Women in Your Life: Redefining Your Relationships

A central task in life's second half is to find ways of living with others, especially your life partner, and to redefine these relationships. We go through significant gender role changes because the male and female second-half journeys can be quite different.

Changes in Gender Roles and Relationships

Robert says, "I feel insignificant to the women in my life. There was a time when roles were clearer. I worked for the financial needs of the family. My wife took care of raising the children. Now, she is working, especially after I was laid off from my job. It is so confusing. She seems to be turning into the old me, and I am turning into the old her."

As we age, many shifts take place in gender roles. In life's first half, each gender adds characteristics that distinguish it from the other gender. However, in the second half each gender completes its development by taking on characteristics previously associated with the other. As women age, they begin to be more interested in tasks and accomplishments than in nurturing. Women across cultures age by becoming more assertive, managerial, or political. While women seem to remain identified with being female, caring for young children and conflicts between childbearing and career achievement no longer diffuse their focus (Sheehy 1998, 319).

At the same time, men show greater interest in nurturing, in expressing themselves artistically, in appreciating their surroundings, in growing in wisdom, and in exploring the spiritual journey. Whereas women seem to become more independent and assertive, men typically become more expressive and emotionally responsive.

Now don't start applauding yet. Not all men take part in these gender role changes, according to Gail Sheehy (1998). Many of the over-forty-five working-class men in the Sheehy survey did not have much intimacy in their marriages. They were resistant to admitting problems that might stigmatize them as less of a man. It was rare for them to have friends they could confide in, and most still were not interested in closer relationships. Their sex lives reflected this increasing distance from intimacy. These are the men on the embittered journey discussed in chapter 1.

On the other hand, the wise men, the men with a higher sense of well-being, spent more time with their spouses, an average of six hours total a week. They were more involved with friends and spiritual pursuits. At the end of the day, they enjoyed a newfound relationship with their partners, with significantly changed roles. The Sheehy survey (1998) found that many older men had changed their perception of gender roles, turning toward compassionate, community-building causes rather than the competitive pursuits of their youth.

Answer these questions in your journal:

☒ In what ways has your gender role changed in the past decade? How has your spouse's or partner's gender role changed?

☒ What role changes might happen to you and your partner in the future?

Men and Women in Relationship

Married men live longer! Men from the ages of forty-five to sixty-four who live with their wives are twice as likely to live another ten years than their unmarried counterparts (Sheehy 1998, 335). Being married remains the strongest link with male survival, even after one accounts for differences in income, education, and risk factors like smoking, drinking, obesity, and inactivity (Vaillant 2002). As studies have confirmed, there is something special about wives that seems to provide men with a cover of protection from depression (Sheehy 1998, 235).

On the downside, one of the unmarked revolutions since the 1970s is the resistance of women in midlife to remarry. The ranks of women divorcées between forty and fifty-four have radically changed from the ubiquitous "dumped middle-aged wives" of an earlier generation (Sheehy 1998, 236). Women now are choosing to remain single rather than sacrifice their independence. But what turns out to be a divorce springboard for many women represents a slippery slope for many men. Middle-aged men seem to be reluctant returnees to single life. In Sheehy's interviews with divorced men forty to fifty-four, the common theme was a sense of downgraded self-worth. Often, these men confessed that their wives instigated the divorce. Further, many divorced women now turn to long-term friendships instead of marriage. Men, on the other hand, usually do not bring long-term friendships with them from their earlier life. Therefore, many become embittered or find themselves in unsatisfying, rebound relationships just to be with a partner (Sheehy 1998).

Half of all single American men between forty-five and sixty-four live alone, but among these who do share a household, it is usually with women to whom they are not married. This is true for two-thirds of men up to the age of sixty-five, according to Census Bureau figures (Sheehy 1998, 157–59). Women over forty-five without spouses are very likely to live with other relatives. Many unmarried, widowed, or divorced females between forty-five and sixty-five are living with men, and they have no plans to marry (Sheehy 1998, 340). Others turn to celibacy, self-gratification such as masturbation, or recycled old boyfriends. Whatever course is taken, the net result is fewer women over forty-five choosing to remarry.

Since men with solid relationships with women live longer, it is important to assess the quality of your relationships with the women in your life. Answer these questions:

- Who are the primary women in your life? Your wife, girl-friend, a grown daughter, other female relatives, friends, or work associates? How would you describe these relationships? Do you have any close female companions with whom you share your inner secrets?

- What is lacking in your relationships with women? How could these relationships be different? What do you need to do to bring about these changes?

- Does your current relationship allow you to experience vulnerability, comfort, openness, and trust?

- Can you say, "I like women's company. I like to talk to them, but I don't feel compelled to be intimate with them. It is now more about affection and vulnerability than simply physical performance"? Can you say, "I don't feel like chasing women anymore. It is not a natural instinct, the way it was when I was younger"?

Redefining Your Relationships with Women

In life's first half, you likely became infinitely ingenious at finding ways of being unhappy in relationships. In recent years, male and female relationships have been, to say the least, problematic. If we are to get through the second half, we have to get beyond gender wars and bashing and find new ways of redefining our relationships one to the other. It is time to discover the sweetness of ripening relationships, to experience the fruits of life's changing roles. Rather than continued criticism of the other gender or simply trading places with your partner, you can become freer to express yourselves mutually, to reach a point where the tensions between you and your interpersonal differences relax at last. You can develop mutual interests, expanding the intimacy you experience.

When you begin to enjoy nature or landscaping, take up a musical instrument you once loved, study a language, explore spiritual realms, it is obvious that a major reorganization of your life is in progress. Instead of fighting life's changes, you can find new roles, tapping into new sources of energy and pleasure that are naturally available to you and your partner. You can become more open to new experiences and reinvigorate your senses, adding new flavor to life. Don't equate your expanding aesthetic interests with being feminine. By allowing yourself to stretch well beyond your narrow stereotype of masculinity you can revitalize your relationship and add more luster to your middle and older life.

Matt, age fifty-five, says, "It seems that ever since I took up playing the trumpet again, which I played in my youth, my partner and I get along so much better. Coincidentally, it seems we go for walks after work more, we share reading novels together, and we have swapped roles: I cook and she cheers for the New York Yankees. Life is good!"

Developing new relationships with the women in your life begins with these steps:

Step 1: Move across the barriers between women and yourself that are caused by sexism. Both genders need allies in the struggle to stop what is hurting themselves and each other. Reconciliation begins by seeking to understand how the women in your life feel, what they want and don't want.

Step 2: Life's second half is a time to be comfortable with women by putting aside your anxieties about sexuality. Life's second half is also a time to be honest with yourself and women about what you truly want.

Step 3: Instead of seeking to be powerful, this is a time to be vulnerable. If men have the feeling of power and women have the power of feeling, perhaps it is time each gender exchanges these roles, to the point where each achieves better balance and harmony. Be vulnerable with the women in your life.

Here are some affirmations to assist you in redefining your relationships with women:

- I will stop underfunctioning in the physical, emotional, and relational areas of my life with women and stop asking women to do more than their share.

- I will stop overfunctioning in the physical, economic, and sexual areas of my life with women. I will redefine my relationships with women by seeking ways to encourage gender role changes over time.

- I will develop one spiritual friendship with a woman in the next year.

- Try saying this to the women in your life (as appropriate): "Today we begin again. I look at you and see a person trying as best you can to live, love, and be loved. Today I see you again for the first time. When we hurt each other, it is because we are each hurting. Today I will try to love you anew. This love will not be easy to give or receive, but I am willing. Come with me on this journey in life's second half. Grow old along with me."

Male Friendships

An inevitable sorrow of living longer is the diminishing circle of peers—colleagues and friends. You lose friends over time due to geographic moves, job changes, illnesses, and deaths. Bob is a long-term and long-distance friend since my days at Princeton in the

1960s. He is the only person with whom I still have contact who knows my past during those troublesome years. I fear if I lose that relationship, through death or benign neglect, I will lose a part of myself. There will be no one else who has that collective memory and shares that past. Who are the key male relationships in your life that you've lost over time? Who are the male keepers of the legends and memories of your past?

The hunger men have for connection with other men has been growing exponentially throughout the years, perhaps silently and secretly within you. For most men, their hunger is not satisfied. If you doubt that, look at how many close male friends you now have in comparison to the number you had twenty years ago. Most men have fewer male friends than before. What male friends do you confide in about almost anything? Tom says, "I was shocked to realize I have not developed a single close male friend since college." Have you? How many new males have you drawn close to in the past ten years?

What has gotten in the way of your developing more close male friends? Lack of time? Other priorities? Work pressure? Family activities? Competition with other men can be a divisive force among us. Competitive activities often result in alienated personal relationships with men, creating win-lose, either-or thinking that pits one against another.

Steve, age sixty, says, "It does not take much for me to feel competitive with another man. I look at the kind of car he drives, and I compare it to mine. Other guys make more money than I do, and I feel envious. Get me on a basketball court and I become Attila the Hun, doing almost anything to win. What is it about men and competition?"

The area of greatest competitive vulnerability for men usually is money. Talking about income is the final taboo between men. A man will never ask another man how much he earns. Instead, there are subtle ways of getting at this information, such as your job title and functions, or your place of employment. Men use status symbols to measure themselves against other men—the kind of car you drive, how big your house is, the clothes you wear. Competition about money is the great dividing line between us.

The relative lack of competitiveness between men and women has enabled some men to be more open and vulnerable with women than with men. Robert says, "I don't have to compete, play games, pretend to be something I am not with my women friends. I can be myself with women because we are not competitive over jobs, careers, money, or status."

It is time to grow out of this destructive competitiveness among men, whether it is centered on sports, salary, or penis size. Put aside your youthful drive to be superior to other men. Choose well your friends, for in the end you will become like them. If you are to have healthy, open relationships with men, you need to call a moratorium on the competition that too often characterizes your relationships with other men.

To develop healthy male relationships requires establishing new patterns of relating to others, to find *philia,* "friendship love," with a mutuality that demands equality. With a spiritual friend, you can let down your defenses, show your less-than-perfect self, let go of the need to be right, and entrust your friend with your heart. A spiritual friend offers a safe place to try things out, to stretch and grow, to not feel shame no matter what you might say. Spiritual friendship demands candor, but it is always truth spoken in love. Trust is the foundation of spiritual friendship, and guardianship of feelings is a primary duty. Intimate friendship is an opportunity to know and be known more deeply.

Here are commitments you can make to yourself when seeking *philia* with another man:

- I will stop competing with, ridiculing, and otherwise hurting other men.

- I will make space and time in my life for male friendships.

- I will become a good listener to my friends. I will actively identify with, care for, and think about men similar to and different from me.

- I will be sensitive to the fact that other men have the same fears of emotional and spiritual intimacy with men that I do.

- I will cultivate what Dietrich Bonhoeffer (1954) called "the grace of interruptibility," the willingness to make time in the midst of life for a male friend.

- I will not let homophobia prevent me from making friends with men, and I will actively oppose the violence and hatred directed at gay men.

Ask yourself: What intimacy do you want that you do not now enjoy with other men? What risks are you willing to take to seek it?

How Supportive Are Your Support Systems?

Research has shown that problems in aging appear to be more related to the strength of your support systems than to the severity of the crises you face (Vaillant 2002; Hardin 1992). A primary task in the second half is to deepen your support systems, the people in your life (besides your partner) who will help you through problems. Instead of thinking of your family and blood relatives as your primary source of nourishment, find different levels of friendship that can fill your life with significance.

Exercise: Your Support System

First, who is part of your support system? Friends, extended family? Now answer these questions concerning them. Give a rating of 1-5 for each question using the following scale.

1—strongly disagree	4—agree
2—disagree	5—strongly agree
3—neither agree nor disagree	

1. I can usually contact a friend when I need support.	
2. My friends check in on me periodically, especially when they know I am going through a rough time.	
3. My friends remember the details of what I am going through.	
4. I feel comfortable and safe when I am with my friends.	
5. These friends respect my needs and requests.	
6. My friends and I have similar outlooks on life. There is a mutuality about our relationship.	
7. My friends and I take turns sharing equal time to talk. Our conversations are rarely one-sided, focusing more on one or the other, unless one of us needs help.	
8. My friends allow me time to talk about the issues I am working through.	
9. I feel energized when I am with my friends.	
10. I feel heard when I share my thoughts with my friends.	
11. I can discuss difficult topics and personal issues with my friends.	

12. My friends are straight with me when giving feedback.	
13. My friends give advice only when I ask for it. They support my decisions and help me take the actions I need to take.	
14. I feel comfortable expressing all my emotions around my friends, such as anger, fear, sadness, hope, joy, and excitement.	
15. My friends understand what I am going through.	
16. My friends allow me to be where I am in the transition journey.	
17. My friends give me insight that helps me see things from new perspectives.	
18. My friends and I celebrate good times together.	
19. I feel I have a good, solid, reliable support system.	
Total Points:	

Scoring

Now, add your ratings. If you have between 75 and 95 points, you likely feel well supported by friends and family. If you scored between 51 and 74 points, you feel some support from friends and family. If you scored between 40 and 50 points, your support system may be of moderate help to you, but you may need others in your life. If you scored below 40 points, your interactions with your friends and family may be doing more harm than good. Take a good look at why you are relying on these people for support. Seek out others who can give you the support you need.

How can you grow your support system, especially with all the time pressures you are under? You need to be intentional about your time with others. Here are some ideas: Reach out to those who attract your attention. Meet for coffee. Go for a walk. Invite a friend to a lecture together to facilitate exchanging thoughts and feelings. Join a support group. Seek the professional help of a therapist, a spiritual director, or a guide. Seek people with whom you can share hobbies, special interests, crafts, artwork, exercise, singing or playing music, or prayer. Join organizations that support causes you believe in. Become part of a faith community. Offer to help out at a social service center in your town. Go to places where healthy people gather.

Once you have found a few people who may become part of your new support system, ask them to sit with you and discuss these issues and questions: "I have all these ideas floating around in my head. Do you have some time to sit and listen to me? I have come up with some new ideas based on my insights. Can you connect the dots with me? Would you share your thoughts with me? Will you help me think of the ways I might benefit from this situation? Will you listen to me as I tell my new story for the first time?"

If you are on the other end of the questioning, if you are a supporter of a person going through these questions, allow your friend to be confused. Listen as they share their foggy chaos. Resist the urge to problem solve, which we men do so readily. When asked to help make sense of something, offer ideas but do not analyze or interpret what you hear. Be a catalyst to stimulate insight. Encourage your friend to express feelings. Don't belittle or dismiss their feelings with trite phrases such as, "Don't worry. It will be better tomorrow," or "What are you so worried about? Plenty of guys have gone through what you are going through." Give them permission to trust their instincts, to find their own way of changing. Support them in putting a plan into action. Celebrate with them and help them learn to enjoy their success by staying in the present moment.

Sex

Sexuality is a critical issue for most men in life's second half. In your youth, you probably sought to have a permanent erection from the age of eighteen to forty. But as you entered your forties and fifties, the old "talking frog" joke holds true. An older man is walking down the street when he hears a frog talking. The frog says, "If you pick me up and kiss me I will turn into a beautiful woman." The man picks up the frog and puts it in his pocket, to which the frog says, "Aren't you going to kiss me? I'll turn into a ravishing woman and you can have me all you want." To this the man says, "No, I'd rather have a talking frog in my pocket."

In *City Slickers*, Billy Crystal and his buddies bemoan the staleness of monogamous marriage. One of them jokes, "Have you noted the older you get, the younger your girlfriends get? Soon you'll be dating sperm!" One of his pals is married to a twenty-four-year-old underwear model, but even he complains it is like having eaten all his life from the variety pak and now it's the same cereal every day.

"And then you wake up one morning and you are just not hungry anymore." Another buddy says, "You can't get an erection."

Sex in the second half can be a troublesome issue for men. Research shows that half of all American men experience impotence at least once after turning forty. For men over forty there are significant changes in the occurrence of moderate impotence, meaning a problem with attaining and maintaining an erection half the time. Problems of declining sexual potency affect nineteen million men over forty in the United States (Sheehy 1998, 186–87). Data from a British study showed that by age seventy the prevalence of complete impotence triples to 15 percent (Sheehy 1998, 186). Nearly a third of all British men over fifty do not have sexual intercourse.

Does this mean the average male can expect the decline and fall of the phallus as a natural insult brought on by aging? No. First, the decline is gradual, and, in a man without major physical problems, there is enough of a threshold of male sex hormones to allow him to enjoy satisfactory sexual functioning well into his seventies and for some men well beyond. Sheehy found that 40 percent of normal, healthy males remained completely potent at age seventy (1998, 185). The 1993 *Janus Report on Sexual Behavior* confirms that nearly 40 percent of men age sixty-five and older functioned well, having sex a few times a week. The likelihood of erectile dysfunction increases with age but is not an inevitable consequence of age alone (Sheehy 1998, 185).

Physically, testosterone levels begin dropping gradually, normally at about 1 percent a year after age forty. A protein called sex hormone binding globulin (SHBG) begins binding up more of the available testosterone. For some the penis begins growing sluggish. Other physiological factors affecting sexuality are heart disease, hypertension, and diabetes. From an emotional and social perspective, several key lifestyle factors can affect sexuality in this stage of life: smoking, heavy alcohol intake, and depression.

Now I know there are some reading this and saying, "Not me. I am as great as ever." It can be difficult to admit to these physical and emotional changes. Yet, although questions about your sexuality may feel personal to you, it is helpful to confidentially review recent changes in your sexuality.

Answer these questions in your journal:

☒ What physical changes have you noted recently in your sexual performance?

☒ How frequently, if at all, have you experienced impotence? To what extent are you concerned about changes in your sexuality?

☒ On a scale of 1 to 10, with 10 being the best sex you have ever had and 1 being the worst, how would you rate your current sexual life?

It's Not Just about Your Body

There is a definite mind-body link in sexuality for men. The plumbing may be fine but your mind and outlook on sexuality and your partner may not be. Sexuality and aging is not necessarily just a medical issue. Attitudes that may get in the way of your addressing sexual concerns are "It is not going to happen to me," "My body is bulletproof," "It is too late to make any big changes in my life sexually," or "The state of my sexual potency is nobody's business but mine. I don't want to talk about it."

As you age, the old thinking, "I can accelerate from zero to a hundred miles an hour in thirty seconds," doesn't work. Carl Jung, the psychoanalyst, described his experience by saying, "I'm like an old car with 250,000 miles on it, but I still can't shake the memory of the 200 horsepower my engine once had" (Jung 1972, 516).

In your thirties and forties, you may have had periods of dutiful sex, when you and your partner were trying to conceive. Sex became a chore. You may have faced career competition (work that took you away from home or kept you at the office late into the evening) and interruptions of young children in the house during what would be sexual playtime. By the time you got home from a long day at work, played with the kids, and put them to bed, you and your partner were too tired to do anything sexually. Sex was buried under efficiency and the desire for a good night's sleep.

These interruptions in your sex life may have taken a toll on your sexuality. Now, in your forties, fifties, and beyond, you face life on the senior tournament circuit, where sex is affected by life's changes. So by midlife you may have entered the "surfing" sex period when sexuality becomes a recreational sport. This runs contrary to the popular culture that assumes sexuality stops somewhere around age fifty-nine. After all, fifty-nine or younger is probably the age your parents were when you doubted that they were sexually active any longer.

Although the prevailing myth about sexuality is that people over sixty are no longer sexually active, studies show that nearly half of all men in that age group still engage in sex. Among those who do, the vast majority said that maintaining an active sex life is an important aspect of their relationship with their partner. Three-quarters of the sexually active men over sixty said they enjoyed as much if not more emotional satisfaction from their sex lives than when they were in their forties (Sheehy 1998, 184). However, sexuality is redefined from the race-horse gait of your twenties and thirties to the slower trot of an aging stallion, when grazing in the pasture and snuggling sex become more appealing.

Jonathon, age sixty-five, said, "My partner and I are happier than ever in bed, with little pressure to perform anymore. Having an orgasm is not the goal of sex. We lie together in bed, snuggle, kiss, and caress in a loving way. Sexually we are more alive than ever."

Second-Half Sex

To have a more fulfilling sex life in the second half, there are changes you can make.

Step 1: Patience is pivotal. In your thirties and forties, your sexual responses hopefully slowed just enough for you to prolong and savor each erotic encounter. But in the second half, the amount of time you must wait after ejaculation before you can become fully aroused again noticeably lengthens. If you remain committed to the penis-as-performer attitude, it will eventually fail you. With patience, if you maximize the time you enjoy intimacy before you have an orgasm, your sexuality will contribute to your energy rather than deplete it.

Step 2: You no longer have to prove yourself as a young stud. Nature provides you relief if you are patient enough to take your place in the cycle of generations. If you cultivate new roles and a new sexual identity, if you savor the freedom to explore the world with a partner, and if you find a deeper spiritual companionship, you will be well on your way to redefining your relationship.

Step 3: It is time you graduate to "surfing" sex. Imagine yourself riding the waves of love. Intimacy and stroking can be enjoyed in the ebb tide. You go up on the next pleasure wave and down in the rest cycle. You and your partner lie there holding each other until you feel the next wave of sexual energy starting to rise again.

Physical changes can be addressed through hormone- and testosterone-replacement therapies. Also it helps to change your lifestyle: stop smoking, go on a diet, lower your cholesterol level, reduce alcohol consumption, reduce hypertension medications, and lower your stress levels. So many men (and women) take anti-depressant medications like Prozac, Paxil, and Zoloft, but these drugs commonly reduce sexual arousal and it is advisable to consult with a doctor about the benefits of these medications versus the potential sexual side effects.

Answer these questions in your journal:

☒ How have you transitioned recently to a more mature form of sexuality?

☒ On a scale of 1 to 10, with 10 the most patient you can be and 1 indicating highly impatient, to what extent are you patient with your partner?

☒ What changes do you still desire to make in your sex life?

☒ Are you prepared to make changes in your lifestyle to enjoy sex more?

☒ What impact has your spiritual journey had on your sexual life?

Conclusion

There is a high price for love and relationships, for they require a change of attitude. The payoff is nothing short of new ways of loving. To gain this reward, you need to create a world where you can love, laugh, and work together without fear of judgment; a world of celebration, not accusation and apology and unexamined assumptions. The women and men you have loved are not your memories, they are your presences.

Chapter 5

Fatherhood: Being an Adult Son and a Mature Father

The father-son bond is one of the most significant relationships in a man's life. It is essential in life's second half that you explore this relationship, whether your father is alive or deceased, to understand the role that your father has played so far, and how you may be suffering from the vacuum of the "father hunger." If you are a father, it is also important to explore how to be a spiritual father to your children.

The Father Hunger

Some men grew up without a father's love, understanding, and affirmation, so they feel a need for approval. Boys seek this affirmation from coaches, ministers, scoutmasters, teachers, and anyone who will offer it. Men seek their father's approval in the military and the business world, and from women. To gain affirmation a man becomes a good team player, the tennis star in high school, a good student, a loyal soldier, or a successful employee. When men are engaged in

macho games, whether of fitness, sexual prowess, or business success, they may be trying to show themselves and others (especially
their father) that they have made it and that they are acceptable.
They try to prove their value in how much money they make. But
the continuous running from one accomplishment to another only
proves that they have not made it and at some level they feel their
own incompleteness. Their self-worth is never clear. The constant
search for earned worth shows. When all is said and done, an inner
sense of unworthiness is evident.

Many men cannot be themselves as men because they are
always seeking to be their father's boy. The problem is that this
pursuit is unattainable and insatiable. This father hunger has
resulted from not having a father—because he either has died, left
the family, or was detached from daily life because of work, addictions, or just plain neglect. He may have stayed aloof from involvement with his children. The result is likely a deep hurt existing
internally within the child that leads to a poor sense of one's own
center and boundaries and a mind that is disconnected from one's
body and emotions. It results in the passivity of an unlit fire. A man
may be on fire, running around seeking accomplishments. But it
likely is a false flame, fueled out of insecurity and not strength.

Without role models a man may be uncomfortable as a man.
Not seeing how his father related to his feelings, a man may have
become awkward with his own feelings. Not knowing how his father
related to other men, other than in competitive activities, he may lack
a true sense of interdependence with other men.

This father-son alienation has not always been as intense as it is
today. But we cannot assume that down through the ages all men
had happy and wholesome relationships with their fathers. Many
fathers were likely abusive and violent as well. But, generally, before
the Industrial Revolution, boys commonly grew up in a close working relationship with their fathers. They worked on the farm or in the
family business along with their dads. They learned the craft of their
father, making a contribution to the family's well-being by helping
out.

How the father-son bond changed over time is secondary; the
important thing is what you recall as a son from your childhood
and your relationship with your father. I fondly recall as a boy
going to Ebbetts Field with my father to see the Brooklyn Dodgers
play. To this day my dad does not have this recollection. This is an
important lesson about the father's impact on the son: it does not
matter who your father was or what you did with your father.
What matters is who you remember he was and what you remember doing together.

Exercise: My Father

Open your journal and explore the answers to these questions about your father and you.

- ☒ Imagine your father standing in front of you now, whether he is dead or alive, even if you never knew him, then complete these sentences: "Dad, I needed you to _____ ." "When I think of my father I feel _____ ."

- ☒ What have you blamed your father for?

- ☒ Who were the other father figures in your life?

- ☒ Did you ever feel you were good enough for your father? Did you have a sense that you were able to please him? What kinds of emotions did he show?

- ☒ How has your relationship with your dad affected your view of being a man?

- ☒ Do you now have a need to do better than he did in life—in your career, making money, as a husband, as a parent? Did you or do you want to show him up in some way?

- ☒ Did you try to be a better son to your mother than he was a husband to her?

Grown Men Relating to Their Fathers

Open your journal and write your responses to these questions, especially those that grab you as significant to your experience:

- ☒ Did your father listen to and communicate with you, your siblings, and your mother? Did he take time to play and laugh with you? What rituals did you observe with your father? Did he respect your privacy?

- ☒ Did he discuss his feelings openly with you, your siblings, and your mother?

- ☒ Did your parents like each other and get along?

- ☒ Did your father admit to having problems? What were the family secrets and forbidden topics that you never discussed?

☒ Do you remember ever being held by your father? If he ever put his arms around you, did you feel safe? Did you trust him? Did you feel that he loved you just for being you?

☒ What was the most important thing your father gave to you?

☒ Is your father the same father that your brothers and sisters experienced?

As you look over your answers you may be aware of a pain in your relationship with your father, your father hunger or wound. It is likely that some of these questions may trigger unresolved pain and emotional awareness of loss or neglect. The void you may feel today is likely related to unfinished issues between you and your father. If you dig deeper in the second half, it is important to face your father hunger or wound in order for the healing to begin.

Coming to Terms with Your Father

You can't totally separate yourself from your father, no matter what the circumstances of life. Whether he influenced you positively or negatively, who he was and what he was stays with you. There is something about your father that makes him like no other man. Can you remember standing next to your father? He did not have to say a word; his mere presence conveyed approval or disapproval. His hand on your shoulder was worth more than a thousand trophies. Standing next to your father either allowed you to feel his strength or drained the very strength from you. Standing next to your dad made you feel either proud and tall or small and overshadowed. But it was impossible to not have an emotional response. Regardless of your memories of your father, you must come to terms with who he was and still is to you.

If you do not come to terms with your father, you risk continuing to live your life based on your father's expectations rather than learning what you truly desire for yourself. You risk treating yourself as you were treated as a child or feeling responsible for your father's happiness. You may continue to blame your father for your problems without learning to take responsibility for yourself. You may repeat dysfunctional family patterns without even realizing it. You risk destroying yourself and those you love with bitterness and rage or cutting yourself off emotionally. You will lose the richness and tradition of your family, as well as an important resource at your own time of need. Finally, as a father yourself, you may go to your grave convinced that you were an inadequate father. Every father, however much he puts on an indifferent exterior, will spend his life waiting, at some level, to know that his son loves and respects him. Thus, it is important for you to find your father, your images of your father, and resolve the lingering unresolved issues.

One of the steps to becoming a mature male in life's second half is to let go of the father that you've held onto in your mind, whether you think of him as a sinner or a saint, or whether his image is hazy or sharp. You carry into adulthood the father inside you, that is a mixture of images and memories of how your father was when you were a boy. You relate to your father as if he were still this internalized image, continuing to form your sense of being a man in reaction to this mental picture.

To develop a healthy relationship with your father you must say good-bye to him. Not necessarily to your actual father but to the image you have kept of him. To heal you must let that image go, to let him be who he actually is or was, to say good-bye to the father you think you had. This way you move from relating to him as the inner boy to an imagined father to relating to him man to man.

Exercise: Facing Your Father

Directions

Have someone you trust read this exercise to you or record it, and then play it back on a cassette. Pause between sentences. Sit comfortably, relax, close your eyes, and focus on the words you hear. Pay attention to your breathing and the sensations of your chest rising and falling as you inhale and exhale. Be aware of your body. Notice the areas of your body that are relaxed, and those that are tight.

Meditation

As you become aware of your breathing, imagine yourself slowly walking down a flight of stairs, feeling more relaxed with each step. Something very important is about to happen to you. At the bottom of the stairs is a door. Reach for the door handle. As the door opens, you see a comfortable room with two chairs in it. The room is warm, inviting, and full of familiar furniture. Your father is seated in one of the chairs. Notice how your body feels looking at him in the chair. Sit in the other chair across from your father. This is your father just as he looked when you were a young boy or teenager. Notice his eyes, the color of his hair, his face, his clothing, his shoes, the way he is sitting. What is he wearing? What are you feeling as you look at him? Perhaps it is difficult to look him in the eyes. Perhaps he has a hard time looking directly at you.

It is time to leave the room, to say good-bye to the man with whom you grew up. You will never see him again. What words do you want and need to say to him? Would you express anger, hurt, regrets, thanks, love? Now is the time to say all the things you have long wanted to say to him. Don't hold back. Be honest. Complete this sentence and say it to your father, "Dad, I needed you to _____ ." "Dad, why did you _____ ?" "Dad, when I think about you I feel _____ ."

Now listen to what he has to say back to you. What are you feeling? Now, rise from your chair and move toward the door. Open the door, pause, turn around, and look one more time at your father. What is the look on his face? Whatever else do you need to say? Express it now. One final time say, "Good-bye, Dad." Close the door behind you as you leave the room. Take a deep breath, exhaling completely. Whenever you are ready, open your eyes and look around the room you are in. Orient your body again to the room.

Reflection

Now in your journal write down what you have just experienced. If nothing happened, try the exercise at another time. Write about this experience. How did you feel? Were you able to say good-bye to your father? Was it easy or difficult? What else did you say to him? Does this exercise change how you feel about your father?

Relating to Your Father
Man to Man

To review the things you are missing in your relationship with your father, answer the following questions in your journal:

☒ What do (or did) you want your dad to know about you that he doesn't? What do (or did) you want to know about him?

☒ What is (or was) the thing you like the least about your father? The most? What were the happiest times? The unhappiest?

☒ In what ways are you like your father? How are you different?

Exercise: Writing a Letter to Your Father

One way to help you understand your feelings about your father would be to write two letters to him. The first letter is a feelings letter, letting him know what you feel about him and your relationship with him. While writing you might reveal several deep feelings that you have kept hidden from yourself and your father. The second letter is an emotional-divorce letter. What words of divorce do you need to write? In an exercise above you said good-bye to your image of your father. In an emotional-divorce letter you seek to free yourself from unexamined feelings about your father. It is time to stop caring about what he thinks of you.

Here's an example of an emotional divorce: Ron said good-bye to his father at twenty-five when he broke away from home. He said good-bye outwardly to his parents, established himself professionally, and freed himself from his dominating father. But at fifty-seven he still was not his own man. His father still had a powerful influence on him. In his father's presence he was careful about what he said. He still wanted to please his father. He realized that to be fully whole he needed to get an emotional-divorce decree from his father.

It doesn't matter if your father is currently living, as you likely will not mail the letters to him. If he is deceased, you can adapt this exercise by either talking with a friend about him and having the friend play the role of your father, or by talking to an empty chair, pretending your father is sitting there. To aid you in this process, find out as much about his life and motivations as possible. Your relatives and former neighbors and coworkers of your father may all be excellent sources of information. Old photos, family stories, or even letters from your father might be rich sources of information. This journey to your father is intended as a learning experience for you. The value of the letter is in the writing, not in the response he might make to it. The letters are primarily for you, to identify and cleanse away whatever feelings you have about your father. Do not expect him to be different because you have written the letters to him. Do not expect him to be happy or comfortable as a result of your letters. Remember, the letters are for you, not him.

Let's review another example of an emotional divorce. Bill is a fifty-two-year-old man whose father is physically and mentally failing as he turns eighty. Bill has never emotionally divorced his dad and now he fears it may be too late. In his letter to his father, Bill wrote:

> *Dear Dad:*
>
> *You have been the most significant person in my life, although for years I could not admit that to myself or anyone. And now as you are dying I see how your shadow has haunted my whole life. I have always worried about what you thought of me, what I did, who I married, where I went to church, what I believed politically and morally. I care deeply for you, Dad. I am only now able to say aloud that I love you. But I can no longer worry about what you think of me. I accept you as you are, with all of your strengths and weaknesses. Now I must let go of your accepting me as I am, for I may never get the words of approval from you that I have sought all of my life.*

Bill never sent the letter. But he felt a great cleansing in writing it and seeking an emotional divorce from his father.

Relating to Your Living Father

If your dad is still alive you have the opportunity to relate to him one-on-one. Make an effort to get to know him better. Here are suggestions as to how you can do that.

- Join your father in an activity that he enjoys, such as a sport or hobby. The crucial thing is to do the activity alone with your dad.

- If you live near your father, consider setting up regular dates to get together. You might go out for breakfast monthly or get season tickets to an event. By being a part of your schedule, the date is more likely to actually happen.

- If you live some distance away, plan to spend some time alone with your father on your next trip to see him. Let him know of your intention well before you arrive. When you talk to him on the phone, always try talk to him separately. Three-way calls inhibit meaningful conversation.

Another activity is to take a personal history with your father. Inform your dad of your desire to learn more about his past. If he is willing, find some time to begin the process of mapping out a family tree with your father. Using a large pad and a tape recorder, record your family tree. A tape recorder helps capture the richness of your dad's stories for you and future generations to enjoy. Use photographs and movies to encourage your father to tell you the family stories. Ask your dad to select photos from various periods of his life to help describe the stories. Set a series of dates with him to go over photos from each period of his past. Ask him to describe a single day from his youth, a key turning point, the high and low points, and influential people or experiences. Finally, take your dad on a visit to significant places in his life. You might visit the places where he lived while growing up, the neighborhoods where he was raised, the family cemetery, or a place where the family vacationed in his youth.

It is best to keep these journeys brief and focused. This is not intended to be an extended vacation with your father but merely one way to elicit his life story and, in so doing, part of your own. A word of caution from my own experience: be careful what memories you unearth in this process. In reviewing your father's history it may raise unpleasant memories that he has tried to repress for years. There is a common therapeutic phrase that applies here: "Don't open a door you cannot close." This means do not uncover any wounds unless you have the time, energy, and ability to bandage the wounds back up. Be careful what questions you ask and what memories you stir up for your father. You may not see how serious the wounds may be for your father (and you) in a given situation. A seemingly innocuous setting may touch off a flood of associations. Proceed cautiously.

Michael has harbored deep resentment all of his life toward his deceased father, Joe, who was abusive to him when he was a child. Michael's son, David, sought to learn more about Michael's history. David sat with Michael and asked questions about Joe. During the conversation Michael became very angry when asked about Joe's behavior. For weeks afterward, Michael was depressed and withdrawn as a result of this conversation and uncovering long-hidden scars.

Exercise: What I Imagine My Father Would Say

Imagine yourself asking your father the following questions, whether he is alive or deceased. Record in your journal the answers you think your father would give to the questions. When you are done with these questions, review your answers and think about the implications of your dad's imagined statements.

☒ Were you proud of me? What about me made you proud?

☒ What most angered you about me? What about me gave you the most pleasure?

☒ What was I like as an adolescent? Was I a good son?

Changes in Fatherhood over the Years

Today most children live with their parents long after they are grown because they cannot afford to live anywhere else. There is now an opportunity for fathers to learn how to nurture their adult children. How do men already in their midlife or older accomplish this transformation? They have to be willing to suspend decades of cultural conditioning and learn how to be nurturers as well as providers. They need to learn the language of the heart; that is, to feel what a child feels and to acknowledge the truth of those feelings, before correcting, punishing, or rewarding. Today, younger fathers are making great strides in learning how to nurture their children, and deriving personal benefits from these life changes.

Contrary to conventional wisdom, fatherhood has as significant an impact on mental and physical health as career achievement does. New parenting research shows that fathers who are highly invested in their work but who also care about their children and spend significant time with them can still have an important effect on the emotional well-being of their sons and daughters and, by extension, on their own emotional well-being (Sheehy 1998, 190). The most promising direction for redefining masculinity is in reinventing fatherhood. Most of the reinvented fathers are now in their thirties and forties. But not all. Many are start-over dads in their late forties and fifties, raising second families. However, the bulk of the early baby boomer men are still stuck in more conventional roles.

Most men in their fifties were not brought up to be warm, sensitive fathers. They could not look to their dads as role models for nurturing. Most were taught to separate quickly from their parents and move away. Many men today did not have fathers who were caring, emotionally expressive, and involved with their children.

There are five major developmental influences that fathers have on us as men. These influences affect us throughout our adult lives. They are nurturing, role modeling, initiation into manhood, mentoring, and becoming an elder. Let's examine these more closely.

1. Fathers are key to the *nurturing* attachments that are critical in early development. Although nurturing is commonly

associated with a role the mother plays, fathers too can nurture their children through expressions of their love.

2. Fathers are *role models.* Children need positive male role models whom they can admire and emulate. Ben, age nine, does not live with his dad due to divorce. When I do projects with him, such as making a model airplane, I glance out of the corner of my eye. I see Ben looking at me, as if to say, "Is this what it means to be a man?" He is searching for a male role model.

3. *Initiation into manhood* is the third influence of fathers. Traditionally, fathers initiated boys into manhood through an experience of the wonders of nature and by facing the boy's limitations. Vision quests and bar mitzvahs were traditional initiation rites. Initiation moves a young man from a natural self-centeredness to a healthy inclusion of others.

4. Fathers are *mentors.* As a mentor the father teaches the boy how to be a productive member of the community. The mentor provides advice, sponsorship, and guidance.

5. The final influence of the father may come later in life as the man moves into the stage of *becoming an elder.* The older father can teach the boy-turned-man the wisdom learned through the ages, to move from aging to saging. The process involves a shift from the outside to the inside, from the physical to the spiritual, and from egocentricity to other-centeredness. An elder plays a vital role for men in their later years but appears to have all but vanished from American life.

The Changing Images of Fathers

Today nearly 90 percent of fathers are present in the delivery rooms when their children are born—a huge increase over the last twenty years. The same study showed that 80 percent of fathers said they wanted to play a greater role in parenting than their fathers did (Sheehy 1998, 59). Since today's fathers want to stay at home for a few days or months with their newborns, by popular demand a third of American companies now offer paternity leave (Sheehy 1998). Most fathers today share the chores of diaper changing and feeding their children. If the husband and wife are still married, it is unlikely that the father will be the sole breadwinner. The wife will likely be working while the kids are still in diapers. With increasing frequency, fathers of young children will be single parents, step-fathers, or living away from their natural children. Some may be the primary child care provider even in intact families (Shapiro 1993).

All these elements combine to offer fatherhood new meaning, quite different from the distant disciplinarian and salary drone of the past. Some of today's fathers have become fully nurturing coparents. The days of the *Ozzie and Harriet* or *Donna Reed Show* dad are over. A new father has emerged in the past twenty years. However, this new father is still more the exception than the rule.

Being a Mature Father to Your Own Children

To make the most of this section, it is time to take a thorough inventory of yourself as a parent up until now, whether your children are young or old, male or female.

Answer these questions in your journal:

☒ In what ways were (or are) you involved in your children's births? In what ways do you feel you matter to your children?

☒ When your children were born, what kind of father did you want to be? Have you been that kind of father to them? How much alone time did (or do) you spend with your children? What rituals did (or do) you have with your kids?

☒ What was (or is) your policy on physical punishment with your children? In what ways were (or are) you a domineering father?

☒ Are you sensitive to gender-related issues with your children? Do you and your spouse communicate at cross-purposes with your children?

The primary focus of this section is being a father to your son or daughter, acknowledging that today there are many other variations of the father-child relationship: the single father, the stepfather, fathers with multiple families, the gay father, etc. This section cannot adequately address all of these variations. But I do not want to imply that fathering only involves the traditional father-son relationship.

By life's second half most men have teenage children in the household. Some men may be early bloomers. By midlife, children may be grown and out of the house. Other men may have decided to have children later in life, even in their forties, fifties, and sixties. Some may have divorced, remarried in midlife, and started with a new, adopted family. A few men may already be grandparents by midlife.

I have always abided by the Bill Cosby philosophy that once kids leave the house, they are never to return. However, I am told that occasionally adult children do return home. It is common today for adult children to return home when they cannot afford to live anywhere else, at least in the style they want. Thus, some men begin parenting again when their adult children move back into the household after divorce or life changes. There does not seem to be a uniform pattern to fit all men. We are all making it up as we go along.

You can help your sons and daughters by sharing your inner life with them, by being open about your feelings, dreams, and fears. As a way of preparing your sons for manhood, you can share the journey you have been through to inform and coach your sons through their own journeys. When your sons get to that stage of their lives, they hopefully will either remember the stories of your life and your struggles or consult with you as to how to see their way through that journey. If your sons received good male energy from you as they were growing up, they are not going to reject it when they are grown.

This list offers qualities about being a man that a father can teach a son:

- How to win and lose with dignity and how to play the games of life without always having to win. How to be a team player.

- How to be with women and other men. How to touch appropriately. How to value one's own body.

- How to surrender, to be spiritual, to pray. How to guide, teach, and lead.

- How to commit to something, such as how to love and accept love.

- How to like oneself, to be appropriately proud of oneself. How to respect oneself, others, and the environment. How to deal with one's feelings.

- How to care, to have hope, and to help others with wisdom. How to find and use power respectfully.

- How to value work appropriately, to have a vocation as well as avocation.

- How to laugh, cry, think, and follow through with whatever has to be done, and how to end things in a careful, caring manner.

Most importantly, your son needs to believe that you respect and admire him, that his dad is proud of him. As he grows into manhood, your pride may seem patronizing if a foundation of praise was not laid in boyhood. What the boy needs all along is not just your parental approval (which most boys hopefully receive), but adult respect and honest admiration. The honoring of the man in the boy is what invites the boy into the club of men. This lets him know that he is his father's equal.

The fearless inventory you took above points you to the father you are or have been, as you perceive yourself. The next step is to ask yourself these questions and record your answers in your journal:

☒ What kind of father do you now want to be to your children? What wisdom have you learned so far in your life that you want to pass on to your children?

☒ How can you find the time and opportunities to pass this spiritual wisdom on to them? How can you be a wise elder to your children?

☒ What kind of help do you need to be the father you want to be? What is your Achilles' heel or vulnerable place as a father? Is it your temper, impatience, or arrogance?

☒ How can you add more time with your children, regardless of what age they may be? Remember, your children need your presence more than they need your presents.

Next, it is time to act. Try the following steps with your children.

Step 1

The first step is to review your time commitments with them. Despite all of the changing images of fatherhood discussed above, even today you may return home long after your infant children are in bed. Even if your sons are still awake when you come home, you may close yourself off by tuning into TV, alcohol, or other numbing behaviors. You may take business trips away from the family for days and weeks at a time.

William, age fifty-one, states, "When my daughter Karen was a child, I traveled for work, one, two, even three weeks at a time. To this day (she is now twenty-one years old) she swears I went away one time for a month, which I never did. But to her, it was a long time, and a month has locked in her head, despite denial on my part."

You may work overtime or work two jobs to make ends meet. One day you wake up and the children have cars and are away from the home in the evening and on weekends. Then the kids get jobs or go to college. Nature seems to play a mean trick on you: the years when your children are growing are your most financially productive years. These are the years of ascent. Yet, by the time you realize that this lifestyle is taking a toll on you and your family, it is often too late. Your children are teens and have active lives of their own or do not desire to spend time with their parents. A family vacation with teenagers can be an oxymoron. You may realize you spent all of these years doing what you were told to do, but lost precious time with your children and spouse, time you can never fully reclaim. You may feel a void as you realize that you have dedicated your life to your career and being a good provider to your family and missed out on the deeper, rewarding aspects of your life and parenting.

What do you need to do to find time for your children? What activities would they enjoy doing with you? What would you like to do with them? Is it time to change your priorities in life, to reorganize your life to become the father you long to be?

Step 2

Is it time for you to do something spiritually refreshing with your children? You cannot give much to your children when you are running on empty. Once you have taken the steps of digging deeper spiritually as this book recommends, you can attend to the spiritual needs of your children. Here are some hints to refresh your spiritual life with your children:

- Find a faith community or spiritual activity that you and your children can share. My daughter Heather and I went for a weekend to a Zen monastery to learn meditation practices. What would work for you and your children?

- Share spiritually oriented books with your children. This can be as simple as reading stories from books such as Jack Canfield's *Chicken Soup for the Soul* series to more profound spiritual writing. Share the poetry of Hāfez or Rumi. Read books with your sons like Richard Rohr's *The Wildman's Journey.*

- Go for a walk together in nature. Talk about nature's wonders, the mysteries of creation, the sounds of silence one finds in the forest or mountains, the sense of awe and wonder nature brings. Talk about your experiences in nature, your spiritual yearning for something greater than yourself, your sense of majesty when confronted by the magnitude of creation.

- Talk with your children about your own experience of powerlessness and the wounds and inner struggles in your life. Be vulnerable with your children.

Step 3

Another action is to heal your wounds through the experience of union with other men. You are not unique. Other men have the same longings about parenting as you do. One of the most profound experiences for me as a parent was when I spent a weekend with other fathers who longed to be better parents. Each man wrote on an index card one thing he regretted doing as a father, something about which he felt guilty. The cards were shuffled and read anonymously aloud by another man. Through sharing with others I had a sense of oneness with these other fathers. As a group we felt that, whatever we regretted doing as a father, there likely was at least one other man who shared the same pain and guilt. Spend time with other fathers or seek out a support group. Talk about the father you long to be. You will learn you are not alone on this journey.

Step 4

Write an ethical will for your children. Much like you would write a will of your goods and possessions, write a will that reflects the ethical, moral, and spiritual principles you wish to leave them. What would you leave behind in the hearts and minds of each of your children? Are there different principles you'd leave for your son(s) than your daughter(s)? What lessons have you learned in life that you'd like them to know? You need not give the ethical will to your children at this time. That depends on their ages. If they are teenagers or adults, you may wish to sit down with each of them and go over what you wrote in your ethical will.

Step 5

Fathers can treat their children as equals, which requires a degree of vulnerability with them. This is a difficult idea for most of us to accept. To allow our children to see the man and father as one, connected in spirit and biology, is one of the central transformations of our relationships with our children. They usually want to keep us on a pedestal (or they have torn us down from that pedestal a long time ago). Younger children want Dad to be Dad and not a peer. But as your children become adults and you hopefully become a wise elder, part of sharing your spiritual wisdom with your children involves vulnerability, as you have seen elsewhere in this book. Being vulnerable with your children allows them to see themselves in you, united in shared humanity and a sense of oneness together.

Conclusion

The first time I sensed equality with my father, I was in my late forties. My father had a heart attack and I visited him in the hospital. As he lay in his bed with tubes in him, an oxygen hose in his nose and monitors above his head, for the first time I was able to acknowledge his frailty and mortality. Like most men, I had always seen my father as virile and active. Now, as he lay helplessly in the bed, he was dependent on others and me to do things for him that he, for as long as I can remember, did for himself. For the first time, I was able, albeit briefly, to share my wisdom with him as to what he now needed to do to recover. How was he to reduce his stress levels and to be less compulsive about things? For a brief time, we were equals and united in a common male spirit. Unfortunately, it often takes infirmity to get to that point.

As my father recovered though, and returned in many ways to his prior lifestyle, both of us lost that sense of oneness to some degree. But those moments in the hospital are memories I will always treasure, as I believe he will, for they were a time of unity of spirit and mind. We were peers, sharing each other's experience, while he remained, and will always remain, my father.

After that experience with my father, I was able to model that vulnerability with my adult children when I was hospitalized over the holidays for severe pneumonia. As I lay in my hospital bed with an oxygen tube in my nose, IVs in my arm, and coughing uncontrollably, my twenty-one-year-old daughter offered me the taste-tempting treat of hospital applesauce. I was dependent on her to assist me in the simple task of eating. We joke now about it, but every time she offered me a spoonful and said, "Dad, you need to eat," I'd say, "I'm thinking about it." But I realize I became, in that moment, the vulnerable and dependent father that I have always been but worked hard to pretend I was not.

Don't wait until you are hospitalized to be vulnerable. It may be too late by then. Do it now. There are many ways to be vulnerable with your children: Share with your adult children times when you have felt weak, powerless, and vulnerable. Discuss with them times in your life when you felt alone, lost, joyful, excited, isolated, or directionless. Talk openly about your fears, hopes, and dreams. Be playful with them. Learn to laugh from the belly and cry from the heart. Tell stories of your life journey. Talk about times when you felt broken. Get in touch with your body and acknowledge your physical aches and pains. Write letters to your adult children from your heart. Tell them you love them. Model for your sons what it means to be a wise and vulnerable elder.

Chapter 6

From Doing to Being: A Different Look at Work

Work, for most men, is that central part of their life that defines them. It is important to take a different look at work, especially in life's second half, to find out anew what you love, to discover a new voice at work, and to act with passion in what you do.

Why You Work

We work because work connects us to reality. We work because many of us have lost our sense of being alive when we are anywhere else but at work. For many, our work is all there is. That is what we do; we work. Remember the scene in *Field of Dreams* when Kevin Costner's character asks the character played by James Earl Jones what he will do after his experience in the baseball cornfield of dreams in Iowa? Jones responds, "I'll write about it. That's what I do, I am a writer," as if to say, "That's who I am, a writer."

Work, what you do for a living, may be how you identify yourself. You may have become your job description. There is a humorous gravestone in London that reads, "Here lies Jeremy Brown born a man and died a grocer." To test this out, go to a cocktail party or a gathering of men. "What do you do for a living?" is one of the first questions men ask each other. In recent years this has also increasingly become the case for women—a big difference from a few decades ago. The question "What do you do for a living?" identifies who we are and is a means of measuring ourselves against others. What you do for a living tells others something about your status in your culture's pecking order. Above all, it is your work that makes you a man among men, which defines your worth in what you think of as the world of men.

Somewhere in midlife you may find you are not what your resume says you are. Perhaps you see that work has become the sum of your identity as you sacrificed everything on work's altar. You are not your profit-and-loss statements or your career ambitions.

Alan, fifty-six, has worked for thirty years as a plumber and said, "My work is my life. I would not know how else to describe myself if not in terms of what I do. In fact, it is frightening to think about my identity after I stop working. What will that be like?"

Exercise: The Lure of Work

Answer these questions in your journal:

Write down how you introduce yourself at a party. Do you talk about what you do for a living? What else do you say about yourself? What is the lure of work for you? Is it the promise of a pension somewhere in the future, the "gold watch" syndrome? Is it the desire still to ascend the ladder of success, the "be all you can be" syndrome? Is it your vision of what you are at work, the "I want to be somebody" syndrome? Is it that the bills still need to be paid, the "I cannot afford to quit" syndrome or a sense that you do not have enough, the "I want it all" syndrome? Is it a sense of self-worth and identity, the "that's how I identify myself" syndrome or access to friendships and social interaction, the "it's my world" syndrome? Or is it a means of tapping into your talents, the "I shine at work" syndrome or the recognition at work, the "here I am somebody" syndrome? Finally, is it a place where you retreat when the kids are screaming and the wife is demanding, the "I can at least hear myself think here" syndrome or a sense of security, the "I'm safe here" syndrome?

You may work to buy the things that you and your family desire, or think you desire. Until recently, we identified our needs and then saved money until we could make the purchases. This gave work a sense of meaning. Work may not have been satisfying, but at least it had an identifiable purpose that was likely appreciated at home, at the workplace, or in society as a whole. Today we seek instant gratification of our needs and buy on credit. Therefore, work becomes merely paying off a credit card debt, detached from the initial purchased item. Today, we may no longer feel appreciated for work done. It feels like a never ending cycle of work and spending: the mortgage, kids' college education, saving for retirement, your toys, and, for some, child support or alimony.

What Has Work Become for You?

In today's workplace you constantly hear the word "excellence." In the eighties, *In Search of Excellence,* by Thomas Peters and Robert Waterman (1988), was the beacon that guided corporations. The word "excellence" was recited as a mantra in strategic plans, mission statements, and goals throughout America's corporate halls.

Instead of being a place of excellence and creativity, today's workplace is a place of power and control that can reduce independence and autonomy. Words such as excellence, productivity, and competition can become your gods, reducing you to a function. You may feel your contribution is unseen and your gifts unwelcome. Although some workplaces have caught the idea that work should recognize the imagination as a vital and essential force, far too many focus primarily on the bottom line and short-term profits.

What, then, can be the toll of today's workplace on you? The greatest proportion of heart attacks in North America in recent years occurred between eight and nine in the morning on Mondays (Sheehy 1998, 37). Perhaps most of the victims were men who found themselves at the low point of a weekly cycle. For them it is as if their human frame is at its most vulnerable when facing the prospect of another week of boredom. Here are the responses of a few men. Tom says, "I am bored in my job. But here I am, fifty-two, and I'll be working into my late sixties. I have a young son who will be entering college when I am sixty-five years old. Retirement? Not for a long time." Carl, fifty-four, says, "I am earning a million dollars a year as a corporate president. I hate my job, but I am scared to death of losing it. If I do, I will not be able to live in the manner to which my family and I have grown accustomed." Stanley says, "I am fifty-eight and have had a good career as a writer. I have no regrets about my career choices. But I have been doing freelance work all my life and now face my elder years without any pension or retirement plan, nothing to fall back on in the future. Now what am I to do?"

There are a number of other tolls that work takes from us. First, work can diminish your life through the practice of self-absence. Your work may have become a problem for you because your sense of your work as expression and imagination may have been replaced by work as endurance and entrapment. What did you do to make your work so small? The problem may not be your work but how you view your work and yourself in relation to your job. You have become your work.

Second, for most of us, work no longer is a place of security. Downsizing, mergers, buyouts, and the transition from manufacturing to service have eroded men's sense of security in their jobs.

Third, you may seek to make work an escape into a world under your control. Yet few report feeling in control at work, especially now when lifelong careers end suddenly with corporate downsizing. Today, many work at meaningless or dangerous jobs because they feel they have no choice. For many, our jobs have become too small for our spirit.

Fourth, from 1980 to 2000, the wage for the average man, when adjusted for inflation, actually declined (Sheehy 1998). In the 1980s many careers exploded with the ever-expanding economy, only to be plunged into the sea in the 1990s. You may now find yourself having climbed the ladder of success only to realize that the ladder was leaning against the wrong building. The safety you were aiming for on the corporate ladder was an illusion. You find that the child for whom you have been sacrificing is grown and gone by the time you struggle back home through the traffic. You feel lost. When this happens, you experience an internal "sticker shock," seeing that the price you paid for career advancement was your vitality, passion, and commitments. It involved the shattering of your deep personal illusions of immunity and safety.

Fifth, perhaps you pictured yourself clothed in pastel golf clothes relaxing all day with your retired buddies, envisioned playing the fairways into your sunset years. You may view your fifties and sixties as a time to give up your contributions as if you had nothing more to offer the world of work. Your memories of work may be more precious than your future energies, referring more to what has been than what might be. You reminisce about the good old days, the golden time at work when people mattered, when quality was important. The problem is that today's young workers do not care about those long-distant years. Reminiscing only further demonstrates your obsolescence.

So instead you reflect on your net worth and assets. You keep mental tally sheets of what you have accumulated so far. You hire a financial planner to assure you that there is enough for the future.

And if you don't have enough, the planner, for a fee, helps you set aside what is needed so you can feel secure.

When you are in your twenties and thirties your work is characterized by a hot-from-the-fire creativity. But by midlife you may feel burned out. Author Sam Keen (1991) says we don't burn out, we "rust out." Burnout happens when there is too much fire on the stove and the pot gets scorched from the heat, as in the heat of youth. Rust-out happens when there is no fire or passion left at work. So your work has become a place of little fire and passion. You have become your own bottom line of assets and net worth.

Are any of the following causing you to feel "rust-out" in the workplace?

Competitive pressures: Do you feel you have to do more to gain someone's approval because someone else is right behind you desiring your job?

The corporate culture: Does work demand that you put in extra hours on evenings, weekends, or holidays? Do you feel you live in an addictive world that is always demanding more of you? Do you feel as if you have to do more with less?

The need to make the numbers: Do you feel the pressure of sales demands, the corporate stress always to do better?

Pressure to serve more people: Do you have multiple customers and stakeholders, each with their own demands on your time and attention?

Rapid change: Are you running as fast as you can but never able to keep up with the pace of change?

Overwhelming work burdens: Do you feel as if there is too much to do and not enough time to do it all?

What has work become for you? Are you rusted out at work? Have you lost the fire and passion you once had? How secure do you feel about your job today?

The Spiritual Journey and Work in the Second Half of Life

By midlife you have worked more years than you have yet to work. From your answers to the questions above, you may have discovered that you have little of the old enthusiasm left for work. You cannot grant it the same degree of life-or-death importance. Yet nothing may have taken the place of what formerly gave you life. In the second half you need to seek new, more profound meaning in your work. This requires viewing work from a different perspective, one that also includes the people and things you have learned to love in life.

Ask yourself this central question: What is the greatest gift I can give my adult children? Is it money, stock, a piece of the business, the promise of a legacy? All are nice things to pass on to our children, but they're not necessary. What is necessary to leave to them? The best act of love you can give your family is to make the effort to stay healthy and alive as long as you can. How do you rearrange your life and lifestyle so that this happens?

You do not live by brains and body alone. You also need spiritual nourishment, to find a way of fulfilling your spiritual hunger. It means coming to terms with what you truly love. It means facing the pain of love, the joylessness of life, the sense of alienation, and the disconnection with feelings that you have carried perhaps through much of your adult life. It means letting these go, turning them over to a higher power. You need to elevate your sense of purpose in being alive, finding that element of soul alive in you that you have perhaps let lie dormant for decades. Your task is to move deeper into another realm of being and to reestablish customs that allow you to find yourself in the world.

Work, in its fullest sense, could be what matters most to you. The art of living well is to accomplish your job without diminishing the priority of your work. A job is something somebody else defines for you. Work is something you define for yourself. You are never fulfilled by your job, only by your work. Your soul is what turns your everyday work events into life experiences, what ignites and inspires you to continue to live.

Work in life's second half is a profound journey of moving from focusing on success to significance, from doing to being. Before, you were defined by your job. Now your spirit and heart will define you. Instead of the journey of ascent up the ladder of achievement, work now is about digging deeper to new sources of refreshment. No matter what you have accomplished or the power and possessions you've accumulated, you are now called to experience life in a new way, to find a sacredness of belonging once again. Belonging means to relate to, to be part of. Spiritual vitality is found within longing, which is at the root of belonging. Work should become that which you long for, where you will find your treasure: be-your-longing.

Work must fulfill your inner needs. As you develop a spirituality of the uneventful, of the low places in life that are neither deep nor exhilaratingly high, work can engage you in ordinary things without being boring. The deepest joys are not the spectacular but the commonplace. Work has its meaning when ordinary things happen to average people in extraordinary ways. The philosopher Teilhard de Chardin wrote, "The value and interest of life is not so much to do conspicuous things . . . as to do ordinary things with the perception of their enormous value" (Teilhard de Chardin 1968, 156-57).

There is a Chinese story that illustrates this point. Once there was a master potter who sought to find a new glaze for his vases, working every day, tending the kiln flames, controlling the heat, and experimenting with new glazes. Nothing created the beauty he sought. In desperation, one day he gave up the struggle and walked into the fully fired kiln. Later, his assistant opened the kiln and took out the vases, now most beautiful. It was the glaze that the master had always sought. The master had disappeared into his work (David Whyte 1994, 114).

In the next chapter I use the term "refirement" to broaden our perspective on retirement. In the light of the above story, perhaps, like the old master potter, we all ought to move to refirement every few years, where we find work that offers a most beautiful glaze. What is the work that would bake you to perfection? What part of you are you holding back at work? Into what fire do you need to walk to become perfectly baked? What would bring fire back into your work?

Work can be the fire where you are baked to a newfound beauty. The fire is yourself fully developed in your work; you become the essential ingredient to make your work meaningful. It is only as you walk into the flames of what you seek that you are able to fuel the transformation of the ordinariness of your work, changing it into a rare and exquisite form. You can have this fire in your work only if your heart and total being are in your work.

To find what brings you joy, you may need to turn in another direction, to the inner reflection held by the image you have found at midlife. This may require a sobering moment of self-reflection. Denny had this moment at the age of fifty-one when he ended an eighteen-year career as a minister of a church to try his hand at writing music. Although he continues to support himself as an interim clergyman, his real passion is writing music. I once asked him, "If someone gave you $100,000 a year and you need not worry about making ends meet, what would you do?" Without any hesitation Denny responded, "Write music." This was his moment of self-reflection toward what brought him joy.

Kevin was a forty-five-year-old lawyer with a successful practice in Asheville, North Carolina. He has never been married and has no children. As he looked into the mirror of his life he asked himself, "Is that all there is?" When he reflected on this question the answer was, "No, I want to give back to society in a different way. I want to work in a helping profession." He left his law practice and returned to school for a degree in social work. He now works in a shelter for homeless men and feels a new sense of significance, not in material terms but in the legacy of compassion he is leaving behind in the lives of the men he helps.

To assist in that self-reflection, answer the following questions in your journal:

☒ How can work be a good servant to your essential nature rather than a taskmaster?

☒ What were you created to be in life? What aspects of your work could you view as fulfilling your destiny and how can you bring that into your work in a way that enlivens and perhaps even scares you a little?

☒ With whom in the workplace can you discuss matters of the heart? If you do not have any confidants at work, with whom do you have such conversations?

☒ If you could take a year's sabbatical from work to reassess your life, what would you do? What would you be that you have never been? Where would you go? What questions would you like answered for yourself during that sabbatical year?

Living Out Your Destiny at Work by What You Say

Is this a familiar scene? You're in a meeting where your boss is looking for an affirmation from all of his subordinates about his latest plan. You have reviewed the plan thoroughly and think it is not a good idea. It will not work. It is too expensive. The boss lays his plan on the conference table and asks everyone to say what they think of it. "On a scale of one to ten, with ten being a great idea, I want your honest opinion of it." He wants everyone to affirm it as a ten. Every subordinate around the table shamefully says it is a ten. It is your turn. "What do you think?" the boss says. In a mouselike voice you say, "Ten."

Perhaps you have, throughout your career, sheepishly spoken or withheld speech because it was easier to go along to get along. Yet, in saying yes when you intended to say no, you sacrificed much of the inner voice, the fire in your speech. Now is the time to find passion in your voice. Instead of the sounds of a mouse dampened by fears and anxiety, you want the voice of authenticity. It is time to face the internal dishonesty you feel when you do not say what you really think. Now you must let your yes be yes and your no be no, to have that passion you have long desired when you speak.

This means to speak from the heart, especially when the tasks assigned you are energy depleting and passionless. This does not mean being insubordinate. Rather, it requires an inner search of yourself for the work that brings life to your spirit. This requires a soul-searching for what it is you truly love to do. When you find the work that brings you joy, you will find the yes in your life as well as saying no to what does not bring you life.

Answer these questions in your journal:

☒ When you say yes, does it sound like a mouse speaking?

☒ When in your life does no blossom into yes? How well do you say no to the things that do not give you life?

Finding What You Truly Love

The men we met above, Denny and Kevin, both sought what they truly loved to do in work. When they had a moment of self-reflection, they found a new sense of significance in work and life.

After I retired from my job in 1999, I was involved in myriad activities, some life giving, and some energy depleting. Friends said, "Seems as if you did not retire but changed jobs," which is perhaps more descriptive of what happens in life's second half. What I learned is to continue to seek what brings me a sense of happiness and contentment. But you must know what you want to be. What is that prize for you? That is the essence of the spiritual journey with work in life's second half.

A barometer of that life-giving or life-depleting energy is your own body. Recently, this lesson was vividly brought home to me. In the winter of 2001, I served as a volunteer at Mother Teresa's home for orphans and dying children in Haiti. It was a profound spiritual experience. Upon return, I became quite ill with severe pneumonia and was hospitalized for fifteen days over the holidays. Although my road schedule of speaking engagements continued (most of which were life giving), I also worked on the love of my life, establishing a training institute on substance abuse with the medical community in China. But my body was not fully recovered. By spring of 2002, I was traveling when my body reminded me that I was tired and running on a quarter tank of energy.

For the first time in my career, I canceled a speaking engagement. At first I felt guilty for letting down my host. But I realized that I needed life-giving work. China is my first work love even though it is a pro bono effort. Anything that threatens my involvement in China makes my world too small and takes me away from the prize.

There was another, perhaps even more important, reason why I needed to cancel the speaking engagement. That weekend Julia, the daughter of dear friends, was being confirmed in church. Earlier, Julia told me that I was one of the three most important spiritual influences on her life. I told her that I would not be at her confirmation, as I would be in another state. Her disappointment was evident on her face. As I reflected after canceling the gig, I realized that family and friends are also a prize for me. Once again, work would take me away from these relationships, as it had so often earlier in my life. I needed now to focus on what is important.

What do you truly love now? Don't give the easy answer: the wife and kids. What gives you life and energy? What is it in your life that is waiting to be born? When you find what gives you life and energy, go after it with all your time, effort, mind, and heart. That is your prize in life. It is what you were created to be.

The Power of Downshifting

Today you may need to find new ways to look at work by downshifting. To downshift is to change to a less demanding work schedule so as to enjoy life more. When you downshift in a car you go to a lower gear. That's exactly what you may choose to do at work. You may need to develop a new attitude about work by shifting into a lower gear.

Do you say to yourself: "I should have left work an hour ago. Between my job and my family, I haven't got a minute for myself. The money is good, but there has got to be more to life than this"? It may be time for you to downshift.

If you wish to see work differently, try the following downshifting steps:

Step 1: Talk to your family about work, what it means to them, what it would mean to live more simplified lives with less resources but more time together.

Step 2: Listen to your gut. What is it telling you about work?

Step 3: Pray or meditate. You need new questions and answers, not so much *how* to work but *why*. To get to these answers, you need time for reflection.

Step 4: Look at your root fears about work, of having enough, the sense of significance you get from work. How can you deal with these fears?

Step 5: Focus on the potential gains of downshifting, such as pursuing a favorite interest, developing closer relationships, and reaching out to others. What is the worst that could happen if you downshifted?

Steps You Can Take to Downshift

Here are steps you can take to change your work pattern:

Step 1: Keep lunchtime personal. Stop grabbing a sandwich at the cafeteria and chowing down at your desk amidst piles of paper and e-mails. Take a walk at lunchtime; eat slowly. The work will still be there when you return.

Step 2: Avoid weekend business travel. Make firm personal appointments.

Step 3: Set reasonable deadlines. Set stop times.

Step 4: Declare your priority for family. This may be hard, as work may have been the number one priority in your life. What would it mean to put family and self first instead of work?

Step 5: Negotiate extra vacation time. Arrange flextime. Go part-time.

Step 6: Make a lateral or downward move. Decline a promotion. Telecommute. Take early or gradual retirement.

Bruce was a successful electrician with a solid book of business. He learned the electrical trade after high school and started his own business in his thirties. He was financially successful, happily married, and his children were grown. Yet Bruce knew there was more to life than money in the bank and saving for retirement. At fifty-eight, Bruce decided he needed to downshift. He met with his accountant and found a way to cash in and access his retirement funds early. He sold his business and bought a house in the Mexican mountains. From there he did electrical contracting jobs in Mexico and the United States. As a hedge against his fear of not having enough, he opened a small business in Boulder, Colorado, and lived half of the year in Mexico and the other half in Colorado. Bruce soon learned that he did not need the Colorado business and that his life was very full living in Mexico. He retired to work only in Mexico.

Bruce downshifted in two steps from a full-time business to more relaxed work. Bruce now picks and chooses the work that gives him energy and passion. He has been an inspiration to many of us.

Downshifting does not necessarily mean that you stop working entirely but that you focus on what you want to do, not just what you need to do. Despite your fears of downshifting, happiness may be discovered in considering all of your options.

The following exercises can assist you in bringing what you love into your work so that you can work with deeper passion. This involves assessing the adequacy of your current career and perhaps making the half turn toward a career change. The second exercise addresses how to go about downshifting.

Exercise: Qualities You Want to Express in Your Work and Your Life

Step 1

Draw a circle and in that circle write down the qualities you can express in your current work. For example, it might be your creativity, your skills, a sense of generativity (passing on to others the talents you have learned over the years), your passion and compassion, or the joys and problems of working with people.

Step 2

Below the circle write down the qualities you would like to express in life's second half. These may be qualities such as expressing love, making an impact on others, leaving a record of your creativity, having a sense of peace, quiet, and joy, participating in a spiritual journey to serenity, or finding more leisure time.

Step 3

Which of the qualities outside the circle can be expressed in your current work? Write them inside the circle above. Which qualities cannot be expressed in your current work environment? Now write these qualities above the circle. As you look over what is inside and outside the circle, mark the three items that are most important to you at this point in your life. The task will be to find how to retain those items inside your circle that are most important and how to discard those items that are not as important. Further, how can you bring into your work those items outside the circle that are most important to you? The essence of work in the second half is to find in work what you truly love to do. When these qualities cannot be brought into your work, you need to find a way to make them part of your life as a whole.

Exercise 2: Your Spiritual Work Journey

Step 1

Imagine yourself setting out on a journey where you are in search of the qualities in your life that you still want to find. Think about both geographic and life milestones as destinations for yourself. Are there places you want to see? Are there adventures you still wish to experience? What areas of significance do you still wish to have in your world? Are there emotional, physical, and social experiences you still want to have in your second-half journey? In terms of work, where would you still like to go in your career? Write down the destinations you still wish to go to, the journey you still want to take in the second half.

Step 2

What do you need for that journey, to take along on this trip? Personal possessions, music to listen to, books to read, people you wish to be with, sacred objects? What other items would you bring, such as social, emotional, and spiritual qualities? List at least fourteen items.

Step 3

Follow the old rule in packing for a trip: take what you have packed and cut that in half. You probably packed too much already. You have more than you will ever need for the your life journey. Cut the above list in half, down to no more than seven items. Having done that, cut it again, down to three items. What are the three most important items you will need for your journey?

Those are probably all you will need for the rest of your life's journey in work. This may be a difficult and painful exercise, casting off the power, possessions, and work prestige you have accumulated so far. But in all likelihood, you do not need these anymore. In fact, they may be an impediment to your second-half journey in the realm of work. Your preoccupation with these items can weigh you down.

Conclusion

In life's second half, you come to terms with the role work has played in your life so far. You need to look out the windows of your life at summer's end, having been busy with everything except harvesting what you have sown. The harvesting you have done has really not added up to much if it focuses primarily on material possessions, power, and prestige. It is now spiritual harvest time.

Be part of what you planted in the first place. Take in all you have and what you have accomplished so far. At the spiritual harvest time you accept that as enough. You do not need any more. Even if you do not feel wealthy or financially secure, you likely have an abundance of things for which to be grateful. The key to spiritual health and work in the second half is to acknowledge and embrace all for which you are grateful in your work life, to find the beauty in what you do by engaging your heart fully in your work.

In *Anam Cara* (1997), John O'Donohue tells a wonderful story about a Zen monk in Japan. The emperor had a magnificent, ancient vase that fell and broke into thousands of pieces. The pieces were gathered up and the emperor summoned all of the best potters in the kingdom to reassemble the vase. One by one each failed and was subsequently beheaded for the failure. Weeks went by and all of the best potters in the land had been killed. One Zen monk remained. His young apprentice gathered the pieces together and brought them to his master. Finally the monk reassembled the vase, and it was truly beautiful. The emperor was delighted and graciously rewarded the monk.

One day, the monk's young apprentice came across fragments of the vase that were never used in the reassembly. He asked the monk how he was able to make the vase so beautiful without these fragments. The Zen master said, "If you do the work that you do with a loving heart, then you will always be able to make something beautiful" (O'Donohue 1997, 160).

May your work in the second half of your life provide you that beauty. May you never become weary from work and may you find, by digging deeper, new sources of refreshment, inspiration, and passion in what you do. May you move from being a human *doer* to being present in what you do as a human *being*.

Chapter 7

Retirement as Refirement

What feelings do you have about retirement? How can you deal with these feelings? Many men are developing a new attitude about retirement by writing a retirement script that prepares them for retirement with enthusiasm and excitement.

What Does Retirement Mean to You?

Retirement traditionally was the square that you landed on in the playing board of life roughly five years before you died. Before the last century, men grew up, went to work, retired, and died. Most men died within three to five years after they stopped working (Dychtwald 1999, 32).

When did sixty-five become the age of retirement? Otto Von Bismarck, at age seventy-four, first set the retirement age at seventy in Germany in 1889, when the average life expectancy was about forty-five. He was talked down to sixty-five. This became the "gold standard" for retirement (Dychtwald 1999). When my grandfather was born in the late nineteenth century, more than 75 percent of men sixty-five and older continued to work. When he retired in the 1950s, half of the able-bodied men of that age still worked. By 2000 the proportion of men sixty-five and older still working dropped to only 17 percent and is now holding steady (Dychtwald 1999). This figure is likely to increase as labor shortages continue and Social Security disincentives to work are removed. In the early twentieth century, a man in retirement might enjoy a paid mortgage, or a trip somewhere while waiting to die. In the twenty-first century, retirement has come to mean different things to different people. Now you could spend 25 percent of your life in retirement. What will you do with the years granted you for retirement?

Today you are offered a range of options for retirement:

- You may choose to retire early on a voluntary basis to do something else with your life. Recall Bruce from the last chapter, who downshifted first and then moved into a relaxed, semiretired lifestyle in Mexico.

- You may be forced to retire early by an employer who seeks younger and less expensive employees. Companies are offering attractive early retirement packages to older employees. Bill was sixty when he was downsized from the power company where he had worked for twenty years. With an early retirement package he was quickly hired back as a contractor at his former company.

- You may retire from one job to begin a second or third career, part- or full-time. This is what I did when I retired. I am more active than ever, doing things that bring greater satisfaction than being a CEO.

- You may not feel as if you can retire because you face college bills for the children for years. You may be fifty and have children in the house under age ten because you chose to have children later in life. Tom is fifty-six and has a ten-year-old son. He will be paying college bills into his late sixties. He says, "When I am able to retire, I'll be too old to do much," which of course is not true but it feels that way when he looks at the distant horizon of retirement.

Danny, at fifty-five, was offered an early retirement package by his company. He was scared by the possibility of not working and of not being important anymore. What would he do when the phone didn't ring and when there were no e-mails for him? Danny's old ideas about retirement meant being "put out to pasture" or "you're no longer needed."

You likely have old ideas about retirement. A common concern about retirement is the fear of losing power and position. When you think of retirement, a feeling of uselessness may haunt you. To counteract this anxiety, many men when they retire throw themselves into other activities—volunteer work, second family, vacationing that never ends, hobbies and avocations—to maintain a sense of having some structure. For a year after I retired, my life was filled with an array of activities. Although there was nothing wrong with being busy, I became absorbed in activities that blurred my purpose for retirement, which was to have the time to explore what I wanted to do, not what I had to do.

For many of us the question is not *when* to retire but what will I *do* when I retire. Answer the following questions in your journal:

☒ What did retirement mean to your father? Your grandfather? In your earlier years how would you have defined retirement?

☒ What images do you have about retirement? Do you see it as being put out to pasture?

Your New Images about Retirement

Today I have new images of retirement, shaped by a radically different work environment. To develop your new images, you need to explore the current messages you are getting about retirement, formed by your current culture and self-image.

The following questions will help you develop new visions about retirement. In your journal answer these questions about what you think of retirement now.

☒ At what age would you like to retire? What will you do when you retire?

☒ What will be your image of yourself when you no longer do things for a living? What are your aspirations now, if any, about retirement?

☒ Do you see yourself working after retirement? Part-time or full-time work?

☒ Is your image of retirement hanging around the golf course or volunteering at the local soup kitchen? What is your partner's view of what you will do when you retire? Will you impose on the lifestyle of others when you retire?

A Different Look at Retirement: The Ideal Retirement Age

Most of the maps in your mind about retirement are out-of-date. Perhaps it is time to retire the old term "retirement" altogether. Today there is a new term, "serial retirement," meaning to retire in stages. Your work and retirement life may go through stages. You may work more at seventy than you did at fifty. You may drop back for a while to part-time work and live on your assets. You may go back to school to learn a new skill at sixty.

What is an ideal retirement age? A recent poll found fifty-four to be the age most preferred, according to Jimmy Carter (1998). Most baby boomers—men and women—say they would like to retire under the age of fifty. Almost none wanted to work after age seventy (Sheehy 1998). Sam, a fifty-year-old successful dentist, states, "I have filled enough teeth in my life. I am ready to stop and do something else, perhaps volunteer in far-away countries where my services are more needed than here in the competitive world."

Now here is the cold slap of reality. For a couple between the ages of forty-five and fifty-four earning a combined income of $100,000 a year, Merrill Lynch says they need to sock away 24 percent of their after-tax earnings, or $18,000 a year toward retirement. That's not counting inheritance benefits. Otherwise they will be forced to accept dramatically lower standards of living during retirement or postpone retirement for a while. The minimum nest egg they need to have by sixty-five in order to retire is $483,460—and that's with a traditional pension—or $660,070 without a traditional pension (Sheehy 1998, 375).

What is your ideal age to retire, without considering any financial issues? In the light of your current financial situation, when do you think you will retire?

Finding a New Sense of Happiness: How to Be Refired

In *Aging Well*, George Vaillant states, "Retirement is highly overrated as a major life problem . . . There is no good evidence that retirement is bad for one's physical health" (2002, 220). The following steps can reduce the problems commonly associated with retirement.

The first step toward retirement is to find a new sense of happiness. You may say you still love your job. But you now need to find a new sense of what you love, defined by who you are and not what you do. When you find what brings you passion, happiness, and love, you will be refired.

Second, celebrate retirement by finding a new sense of meaning in living. What gives you passion? Retirement is a time of refirement and redirection, a time to be open to what is inside of you waiting to be born anew, to find a new, true sense of happiness. In the second half of life, it is not dollars or titles that bring true happiness. It is the quality and quantity of meaningful relationships. Upon retirement, men who describe themselves as having a strong sense of happiness typically take pleasure in their adult children and often turn to them for comfort. According to the Harvard Study of Adult Development, research found that most retired men who were successful in quickly replacing former coworkers with other social networks described themselves as more satisfied with their lives, more fulfilled (Vaillant 2002). Learn to play anew with these friendships. Play can make retirement fun, for it produces a joy that requires neither reinforcement nor reward. Being playful with your relationships should be carefree. Also, seek creativity with your relationships, not in the competitive way of business but in a way that explores your committed and perhaps hidden talents that gives you pleasure and joy. Creativity can come in the form of service to others. Finally, seek continuous learning. "Gusto for education in late life is highly correlated with psychological health" (Vaillant 2002, 246). Vaillant summarizes this process as follows, "Play, create, learn new things, and most especially, make new friends. Do that and getting out of bed in the morning will seem a joy—even if you are no longer 'important,' even if your joints ache, and even if you no longer enjoy free access to the office Xerox machine" (Vaillant 2002, 248).

Third, the comfort of mature love is the single most important determinant of men's happiness in life and especially in retirement. Ninety percent of the happiest retired men are in love with their wives today and say they have grown closer since retirement. In contrast, only half of the unhappiest retired men have become more intimate with their mates. Those who said they were less happy had a long list of psychosomatic complaints upon retirement, chiefly insomnia, broken sleep, tiring early, feeling fat, problems with digestion, high blood pressure, and feeling irritable and angry much of the time (Vaillant 2002, 219–48).

The following exploration will help you find a new sense of happiness in retirement. Answer these questions in your journal:

 What makes you happy? What gives you energy? When you find what brings you joy, you will be refired, not retired. What gives you meaning and passion?

☒ What inside of you is waiting to come out? To happen?

☒ How much of your happiness do you find in your family, children, friends, religious group, or social life?

☒ When you think about what will make you happy in retirement, what would you look forward to each day?

Facing Your Fears

As children we learn how to distinguish between fears of real things (being hurt) and imagined fears (the bogeyman hiding under the bed). By the same token, you need to face your real and imagined fears about retirement. Here are fears you may have and techniques you can use to face them.

You may fear having diminished energy and importance. Rather than accepting your natural limitations of aging, you may push beyond your limits or give up entirely. Give yourself permission to say, "I have less energy. This is an opportunity to grow wiser today. What can this teach me? How do I take advantage of the tune that is now playing in my soul?" Huston Smith, the philosopher of religion, when he was eighty years old and suffering from a painful case of facial shingles, said, "Apparently somebody up there has decided to offer me another teaching" (Smith 2001, 253). Instead of bemoaning the losses you may be experiencing, marvel at what you are becoming.

Perhaps you fear that when you are retired, you will not be expected to contribute to society anymore. You may wonder how you are to create significant connections to your identity when the work connections so vital to you no longer exist. What can you say the next time you go to a dinner party and you're asked, "So what do you do for a living?" Jerry, recently retired, replies, "I am a father of two grown daughters. I am deeply committed to aiding the poorest of the poor and addressing the problems of crime in our neighborhoods." Whatever words fit your present life, use them, instead of defining yourself by your former occupation. When people say, "Sure doesn't sound like retirement to me." I laugh and say, "Now I do what I want to do, not what I need to do."

You may fear change. The key to facing your fear of change is to define a new purpose as the driving force in your life.

In your journal answer these questions:

☒ What do you fear about retirement? With whom can you share your fears about retirement?

☒　What skills do you have and use to deal with your fears about retirement?

Appreciating Your Wisdom

Retirement means that you value wisdom as much as information. In life's first half, you gained knowledge, organized it, and disseminated facts. In life's second half, you gain wisdom and you disseminate that wisdom to others. This is the process of becoming a wise man. The key is to appreciate and value the wisdom you have gained over the years.

Here are techniques you can adopt to aid in appreciating your wisdom.

Technique 1

Allow time for your wisdom to settle within you, to see your natural wisdom. This comes in being peaceful and calm with yourself. It helps to have a daily practice of calm meditation or prayer to sit with your wisdom. Make time to stop and reflect on where you have been so far today and what has been important to you in retirement.

Technique 2

To appreciate your wisdom you may need to make friends with your emotions. An open, empty mind allows you discover a freer awareness of what you are feeling. In retirement you will spend more time with yourself, with fewer distractions. Understanding your emotions will be critical to how you spend your alone time.

As you spend more time in retirement you need to experience your emotions as a living presence instead of trying to control them or react to them. This means facing your shadow and your demons. Going into the turbulence of your emotions is like entering the eye of a hurricane. The surrounding winds may be turbulent but eventually you arrive at a clear opening in the midst of the storm. Step back from what's happening and put your emotions on a stand beside your desk and look at them. Just let them be there, without any sense of right or wrong, good or bad.

Technique 3

In retirement you may not be as physically active as during your working years. Be attuned when your body says to you "time to slow down." With age, energy declines too. At day's end, even if you traveled more slowly, you still are closer to where you wanted to go than at the day's beginning. This acceptance is the true beginning of the wisdom journey.

Technique 4

Don't expect the youth of society to beat down your door begging for your wisdom. Instead, you need to initiate the exchange and remember what you bring to the table. Maybe it's okay to be a bit obsolete. Appreciating your wisdom does not require that others do so as well. In life's first half it was important to be recognized by others. In the second half it should be sufficient that you appreciate your own wisdom without needing anyone else's approval.

It is important to accept that you have enough. In retirement you don't need any more possessions, knowledge, money, and power. You have the ability to share the love you have been given with others.

Come to terms with the "if onlys" that plague you. "If only I had more. . . If only I did this in my career, then I would be happy." This line of thinking keeps you clinging to what should be. Learn to live and rest in the present moment, in *what is*. As the trumpet of desire quiets down in retirement and externally driven pursuits fall away, you have the opportunity to spend more quality time with yourself and to understand the power of your mind. By slowing down and drawing in, you can open yourself to some of the most fruitful experiences and richest gifts that retirement has to offer you.

Now What?

What do you want to do now? Here is a sampling of things to savor:

- I want to sing and dance more.

- I want to visit sacred places, to be more playful and prayerful, to mentor younger men, to live more deeply into the mysteries of life.

- I want to complete my masters program. I want to write a book. I want to take a course in poetry. I want time for woodworking and my vegetable gardening.

- I want to live in a third-world country for a year and work as a volunteer offering humanitarian aid.

- I want mornings for myself, for reading, studying, and writing, to walk in the countryside, and to spend evenings with my partner.

- I want to enjoy my kids and grandkids, to savor old friends, and to find new ones.

- I want to participate in a spiritually vibrant and socially active group, working through religious or community agencies for a greater degree of racial, sexual, and economic justice in the nation.

Ask yourself, if it all ended today, what would be unlived in your life?

Preparing for Retirement with New Practices

These practices can prepare you for retirement:

- Try something new every day. Wendell Berry writes, "So friends, every day do something that won't compute. (Do it for no reason.) Love someone who does not deserve it. Ask questions that have no answers. Invest in the millennium. Plant sequoias. Expect the end of the world, then laugh (when it does not happen). Be joyful though you have considered all the facts" (Berry 1985, 209).

- Part of who you are is who you will be. "So what do you want to do when you grow up?" is the question you ask your children. You ask your teenagers, "What do you want to do when you graduate college?" But in retirement ask yourself, "What am I becoming? What do I want to be?"

- Revel in nonwork activity. Leisure is non-work activity chosen for its own sake. What are you doing that has a festive sensibility to it, like art, sports, or learning? Be carefree in the delight of what you do, like children or lovers at play. Can you see work beyond productivity and find the peculiar balance between doing and being that suits your soul and your season?

- Ask yourself, "What do I have an appetite for? What do I want to taste again or for the first time? What do I want to savor in my life?" In retirement you will have the time and hopefully resources to taste many new things, or old things again for the first time.

Writing Your Retirement Script

It is helpful to envision your retirement by writing a story or a script about what this next phase will entail. This script involves three steps: (1) preparing for retirement, (2) coping with the changes ahead of you, and (3) coping with life in retirement.

Preparing for Retirement

As you prepare for retirement you need to do several things. First, have the confidence that you can face retirement, whenever it occurs. Second, deal with any feelings, fears, or anxieties that might arise. Third, release any tension through relaxation exercises. Finally, focus your attention to the tasks ahead.

To help prepare, complete each of the following statements in your journal:

☒ I know I can face retirement because I _____ .

☒ When I retire I want to _____ .

☒ What gets in my way in thinking about retirement is _____ .

☒ To overcome these fears and anxieties, I will _____ .

☒ When I feel anxious I practice the following exercises ____ .

Developing Your Retirement Coping Skills

When you get closer to the idea of retirement, it is time to remind yourself about the themes in your life. You will need coping skills to help you deal with the hurdles ahead of you. To help cope, complete the following statements:

☒ My physical coping skills and resources (such as a regular program of exercise, muscular relaxation techniques, or breathing exercises) include _____ .

☒ My emotional and psychological coping skills and resources (such as anger management skills, the ability to vent my emotions in a positive way, or a sense of emotional stability in my life) include _____ .

☒ My social coping skills and resources (such as my family and friends around me, financial stability, my home environment, or my community) include _____ .

☒ My spiritual coping skills and resources (such as a relationship with something greater than myself, a higher power, a sense of purpose and meaning in life, or a daily practice of prayer) include _____ .

Envisioning Your Retirement

Draw a picture of what retirement will look like when you get there. This is an important part of facing retirement—envisioning the future. You can refer to the picture whenever the idea of retirement comes to mind. If it is a negative picture, rethink more positively how you would like to have the picture look. Carry the picture with you to work.

Put words to the picture, writing along the side of the paper what positive feelings and emotions you hope to have in retirement. Say those words to yourself on a daily basis. At first it will seem forced and strange—not like you. By rehearsing your emotions you will be better prepared when you need to deal with these emotions and you will expect greater and more positive things to happen.

Conclusion

Retirement can be a time of either decline or refirement, the choice is yours. When you discover your passion and joy in living, a new vision of refirement will emerge.

Chapter 8

But You're Still Going to Die: Facing Mortality

In the first half, you thought you'd live forever. But in the second half you likely have faced many deaths: parents, loved ones, friends, colleagues, people your own age who died well before their time. Facing your own death is part of living. We will all die, eventually. Your days are numbered; you just don't know the count or score. Although your death is inevitable, everything you know about it is theoretical or secondhand. You do not know what the journey of your death will be like until you face it. Although life should be a preparation for death, most of us do not wish to face that final loss.

How We View Death

Paul, age fifty-nine, says, "Death is a mystery to me. I don't know when death will come to me, what there is on the other side (if there is another side), or how I will deal with the pain and suffering which might surround my death. Because it is such a mystery, I work hard to avoid facing death. I even resent it when someone brings up the topic."

If you haven't noticed, your birth certificate has no expiration date on it. Would you want to know that expiration date if it were possible? The reality is, deny it or not, you are going to die. Because you don't know when or how you will die, you live your life as if there will always be another tomorrow to realize your dreams. You may live with the illusion that your death is not going to happen and you'll remain forever young. Our youth-oriented veneer served a useful purpose in the first half: like a faithful soldier, it stood guard at the door, defending the built-in program to live as long as you can.

Death is something that you cannot grasp until you are at its doorstep. You can read books about death. You can sit with others as they die. But you never know what death will be like for you until you experience the shadow of death. You may frame death theologically, viewing it not as the end of life but as a transformation of physical into spiritual life. You can be reminded that the present moment is all you have, but when the last present moment comes, you may be little prepared for it. You may react with the usual responses of denial, anger, bargaining, anxiety, sadness, disorientation, and depression, for it takes time to face death's ultimate realities. You may "rage against the dying of the light," in Dylan Thomas's words. But it is still, in the middle of life, a dark and mysterious place to which you dread going. The sting of death is not fully removed by these reflections, at least not in the second half of life when you realize there is less time remaining on life's clock.

The modern world has isolated life from death. Therefore we have an aversion to and fear of death. We fear the unknown. You may use euphemisms about death such as "passing away" or "going to a better place." You separate yourself from death, as it becomes a detached and emotionless experience. It is because of this sterility around death that images of concentration camps in Nazi Germany or Bosnia haunt us so. The images are too real, too believable. You find yourself both shocked and fascinated by these images.

For philosopher John Paul Sartre, death mocks all distinctions between truth and falsehood, beauty and ugliness, good and evil, justice and injustice, faithfulness and unfaithfulness, success and failure, by reducing them to the same level. If death is the final and defining word, then at that point it seems there is no answer to the question, "And what then?" So you avoid the reality of this final word, believing there is another answer to the question, "Then what?"

We not only avoid facing death, we also fear dying. Woody Allen said, "I'm not afraid of death. It's just that I don't want to be there when it happens." It is the unknown of what lies ahead that we fear most, as death is a collision with the ultimate forces of life. We fear the pain and suffering that may precede our death. What will happen to you in the moments prior to death? Because you fear dying, you cling to the life you have.

Eddie, a sixty-year-old HIV-positive musician, has experienced the accolades of the public. But as he faces the possibility of a painful death from AIDS, he often wonders what death will be like. How will he cope with the suffering that may be ahead for him? What will all of the praise and public acclaim mean to him on his deathbed?

Why Face Death?

Writing about death in a book on life's second half may seem, to say the least, morbid. Why spoil a perfectly good night of reading by reflecting on death? You could say, in a book about digging deeper, that death involves the ultimate form of digging deeper, like six feet underground. In youth-oriented America, speaking of death is not only unpopular but as taboo as sex was in the Victorian era. There is a common misconception that talking about death diminishes your quality of life. On the contrary, by addressing death, you learn to live more fully. To move from success to significance, you must come to terms with your death. You need not fear death. When you are released from your view that life goes on forever, when you face death, you acquire a broader perspective on life and a rootedness in the continuity of time.

To play life's second half, you must explore death and find new sources of life. Facing death means finding meaning in the days granted you. You must look inward to what gives you life, what animates you. Death is an essential part of living. To understand life, you must understand death, for you then broaden your vision of your life. You also will treat life with greater reverence, for to find hope in dying is to find hope in living. In Tibetan Buddhism is the idea that a superior practitioner meets death with great joy. A mediocre practitioner meets death without apprehension. An average practitioner meets death without regrets. All of us can become at least an average practitioner if we view death differently (Rinpoche 1993, 37).

Facing Death Begins by Living in the Present Moment

There are two components to living in the present moment. The first is an awareness of the "last-time" events of life. Second is not grasping at things or even life itself.

You live life in the rearview mirror, seeing the realities of where you have been more readily than seeing the realities of your life as they are occurring. Key moments in your life go by, and you didn't even know how important those moments were until they are gone. So many last times come and go in life without you ever realizing it was a last time. All of the little instances of "lastness" are rehearsals for what lies ahead. Do you remember the last time your mother sang you a lullaby, the last time you sat on her lap, the last time you played with a certain toy or played a particular childhood game? The last time you played catch with your dad? You probably were not aware of when you sat together at dinner with your parents for the last time. As a young parent you may not have known the last time when you changed your child's diaper. You were not aware of it when you went for the last time to the park to play on the swings with your children. Do you recall the last time you helped your children with their homework? The last banana split you shared at a soda fountain? Were you aware of the last time you sat up at night waiting for your teenager to come home late from a date? Do you recall the last high school report card that you painstakingly reviewed to your child's dismay? These last times were likely not known or acknowledged at the time. You only know it now in retrospect, looking back in the rearview mirror of your life. Many of these memories about times as you were growing up may be bittersweet because they signify leaving childhood dependency and protection and the magical fantasy world of childhood behind.

Even now I can close my eyes and transport myself to the bedroom of my infant daughters, Heather and Kiersten, singing the folksong "Hobo's Lullaby" to them. There I sat in the middle of the night, rocking my daughters gently back to sleep after a nighttime feeding. At the time it seemed like a tiring chore. Now I would love to sing one more chorus of the lullaby to them as infants. Every so often, I would like to go back for just a few minutes and reclaim a precious moment of that experience, one last time. If only I had known at the time that it would be the last time.

These ordinary but precious events are little endings or deaths that punctuate your life and remind you of life's impermanence. They are all little rehearsals for your death. When you are aware of the significance of these events in the present moment, you become self-conscious, observing, and savoring life as well as living it.

As you think about the last-time events of your life, answer these questions in your journal:

☒   What last-time events were most precious to you?

☒ Which of these would you like to do over one more time, if possible?

☒ How have these last-time events prepared you to face death?

Living in the present moment means not getting stuck in this life. Buddhism teaches that if you want to know your future, look into your present action. What you will be is what you are. If you fail to enjoy the events of the present moment and get stuck in holding onto what is, you will be the same when death approaches, grasping onto whatever life remains. Death is the greatest teacher, because in facing death you become more responsible to what is, what you do and say, and how to live more fully now. Since life is impermanent, you can free yourself from the incessant grasping at things.

What Death Means

We come into this world as infants, powerless, and we will die powerless as well. As we age, none of us wants to be dependent upon another, certainly not for rudimentary care and comfort. Powerlessness means a falling away and a letting go. Powerlessness is about the inexorable process of loss of self. And death is the ultimate loss of self.

Mortality raises questions about making sense of life, demanding an answer to the questions, Has my life mattered? What was this thing called my life all about? What was its purpose? What will it be like to die? Is there another side to life after death?

Pete, a longtime friend, was dying of emphysema. In 2000, two weeks before he died, I went to California to visit with him one last time. Pete, his wife Bea, and I all knew this would be our last time together on earth. As I looked at Pete carrying around an oxygen tube, taking breathing treatments, showing great pain in his labored breath, I knew he would die soon. I struggled with his death. Was it that one moment he would be alive and the next moment not? What would that final act of breathing be like for him? What will it be like for me when my day comes? What legacy did he leave behind in the hearts of his wife, children, grandchildren, and me? Even as I sought to be supportive and caring of Pete and Bea, I wrestled with questions about the meaning of life and death.

To assist you in understanding what death means to you, it may help to review the deaths you have experienced. Answer the following questions in your journal:

☒ What key people in your life have died?

☒ Have you ever been with a person when they died? What was that like for you? What were your emotional reactions and feelings?

☒ Often your image of death comes through the distant lens of television, movies, and other media. How have these shaped your view of death?

☒ Whose death do you fear the most? What does death mean to you?

Living by Dying

You learn to live by practicing dying. In so doing, you come to see that death is the final stage of your healing. Author Mitch Albom writes in *Tuesdays with Morrie*, "Once you learn how to die you learn how to live" (1997, 32). Let's examine the spiritual steps and concepts for the practice of dying.

1. *You need to learn to number your days.* The Hebrew psalmist wrote, "Teach us to number our days, so we may walk in the path of truth" (Psalms 90:12). He reminds us that we are dust, we shall return to dust. When you number your days, you learn to live in the present moment, soaking up all the life you have. It means that you savor each breath you take, each moment given, and each experience as a gift. It means to awaken in the morning thankful for the new dawning and the twenty-four hours you have been given anew.

2. *The second part of the psalmist's wisdom is "so we may walk in the path of truth"* (Psalms 90:12). To face your death means to face what truly matters to you, your true self, that which you are called to love in yourself and in life. Truth should guide you in the second half. What remains after you when you die? Truth remains. The truth you have lived in your life. The moment of death may not be an ideal time to find out what you believe. It is important that you envision what truth means to you now.

   Buddhism teaches us that we live in illusion that we are a reality. When you see that you are nothing, and being nothing, you are everything. This is the truth of life.

Answer this question in your journal:

☒ What principles guide you in life? What matters and does not matter to you?

3. *It is important to look at what would be unfinished for you if your life ended today.* What do you still want to do? What would go incomplete? Why are you not doing these things now instead of waiting? Do them today! What are you waiting for? Remember, you cannot do all of your life's homework right before the final exam. Rainer Maria Rilke said, "Be patient with all that is unresolved in your heart, and try to love the questions themselves. Do not seek for the answers that cannot be given, for you wouldn't be able to live with them, and the point is to live everything. Live the questions now, and perhaps without knowing it, you will live along someday into the answers" (1981, 211).

4. *You should begin early to practice for your death.* This may be a strange concept, but life itself is a preparation for its ending. Skills for dying well must be learned by the healthy and vigorous. It is time for you to live life to its fullest, to experience the abundance of your life. If you know that you are going to die, if you prepare for your death, you will be more involved in your life when you are living. Conversely, you practice dying by living today. Buddhists believe that you have a little bird who sits on your shoulder and says to you every morning, "Is this the day you are going to die? Are you ready to die today if this is the day?" If you really listen to the bird on your shoulder and accept that you are going to die, someday if not today, you might do things differently. You might not be as ambitious as you are. The things you spend so much time on, such as the work you do, might not seem so important. You might make more room in your day for spiritual things if you listen to the bird on your shoulder.

   Practicing death means to accept the inevitable falling away of the extraneous and coming to terms with your losses. The sum of all the concomitant losses in your life is the loss of a carefully crafted identity that may be tied to your occupation, your family, or your successes in life. When others no longer perceive you as useful, your perceived identity may be lost. By then it is too late, for there is great pain and diminishment in being known only as an old person or a stroke victim or a shut-in.

   To practice for the ultimate loss, you must let your losses be lost. The fruit of loss is simplification and a return to the ground of your being. When you are able to accept loss, you eventually learn not to fear death. Death generally does not sneak up on you. Life gives you ample warning to prepare for your appointment with death. Throughout your middle years, despite the best diet and exercise regime, your body has been reminding you of your mortality through its gradually diminishing energy level, slower metabolism, hair loss, changes in skin tone, and so on. Instead of these reminders paralyzing you, when you accept them, you learn to let go.

5. *Death requires different eyes.* You are more than your actions, your thoughts, your mind, and your body. You are also soul, and therefore you can come to the mystery of death without the sense of fear and dread. Whatever the sum of your life so far, it is important to say, "It's been good." If you were to die today, it was enough. You prepare yourself for dying by spending your days with love and gratitude in your heart for what has been given you. Practice saying to yourself tonight when you put your head on the pillow, "It was a good day. It was enough," without drawing up mental lists of all you did not accomplish today.

6. *Think now about what might lie on the other side of life.* Many religious traditions teach us about the other side—the *bardos* in the Tibetan texts, the afterlife of Islam, the mansions in the Kabbalah, the heaven and hell of Christianity, the ground of being in Buddhism. They all point to a realm that the soul enters after death. Since no one has ever gone to the other side and come back, we must rely on sacred texts that point the way and on our imaginations. What do you believe will be on the other side when your present life has ended? As we will see in the chapter on in-between times, life consists of overlapping endings, middle times, and beginnings. Death is at the same time an ending and a beginning. It is not an absolute ending but merely the taking off of a tight shoe and finding a more comfortably fitting one.

7. *Finally, envision your death.* Write a script of your death drama.

   • Picture your deathbed. How old are you when you die in this drama? Whom would you invite to be beside you at the time of death? Whom would you definitely not want to invite?

   • What would your final farewell to your family and friends be like? What music would be playing in the background? What stories would you like told? What food would you like to consume for the last time? What words would you like to have said? By whom? What would you like to say to others?

In this script, imagine yourself calling on the assistance of a spiritual guide. Picture yourself hitchhiking into the afterlife with your teacher. Envision synchronizing your breathing with your teacher through meditation. You may say, "Into your hands, I commend my spirit."

Being with Others as They Die

An important way to prepare for your death is to be with others as they make their final preparation to die. When you are with another at the point of death, you are introduced to the mystery of death, the wonder of what it may be like when you get to that point. Mirrored in the face of others, you may see reflected what your face might look like at that moment. Buddhist *roshi* (teacher) Sogyal Rinpoche says, "There is no greater gift of charity you can give (to yourself and others) than helping a person to die well" (1993, 186).

Here are some tips for being with others as they die. When you are with others who are dying, it is important to help them put their affairs in order legally, medically, and financially. It is advisable for them to have a living will, releasing their caregivers from the burden of deciding about the maintenance of the body when all efforts are futile. A living will may not be right for everyone, given the relationships involved. Making a will can be difficult for some because of the superstition that as long as there is nothing said about death, they will go on living. But a will is an important step in facing death.

For the dying person, perhaps living as long as possible is not always the greatest wisdom. What about their quality of life as they struggle with pain in dying? Does the person have an image of how and when they would like to die? Where do they wish to die, at home or in a hospital? How can the spiritual atmosphere they desire be created? How conscious does the person wish to be at the moment of their death? What degree of control over their pain medication do they wish to have? Research has shown that when patients control their own pain medication, they need less of it and report less suffering. Other issues to consider: How would they like their body to be handled when they die? Cremated? Buried? Do they want their organs donated to science? Who will be the executors of their will? What would they want done at their funeral? My father-in-law wants a John Philip Sousa march and polka music to be played. I want the New York Philharmonic to play Tchaikovsky's Sixth Symphony and to have Kathleen Battle sing "Pace Mio Dio" and "O Divine Redeemer." (Not too much of a request, is it?) By assisting others in their dying, you are preparing yourself to face these inevitable issues when it is your time to die. Practicing with others is good practice for yourself.

The greatest gift you can give to another is your simple presence. Listen to the dying person's fears and concerns about living and dying. Do not offer meaningless, cheery optimism about death, such as, "It will be okay. You will recover from this illness" or "Dying is simply going to a better place." Such banality denies the reality of the fears and reflects more your own discomfort with the discussion. When talking with a dying person about death, you need not use religious language (unless the person and you are so inclined), but you must be comfortable dealing with such language. You should offer gentle permission to be candid and create a safe place for each other's fears.

Sometimes stories are easier avenues through this process as you allow each other, person to person, to tell the stories of your lives. The spirituality of death is always about storytelling, things in the past and present, offering a time of closure. It is a time for remembering, which literally means "to bring together once again," to re-member. Here are some pointers in listening to another person's story as they face death:

- When you sit with a dying person, say to yourself "Let me be present for this person. Let me put away myself and let me mirror the compassion that I have experienced in my life. Let me not dismiss the other with trite phrases simply because I am uncomfortable with their intense emotions." Sitting in genuine peace with people who are dying has a contagious effect, offering the spaciousness of resting in your soul rather than in your ego. You can lead yourself and the dying person toward silence and their own soul's embrace.

- Let go of your hopes and fears about their survival. Don't take what they say personally. It is not about you, at this point. Put yourself in their shoes. What would you want said or done if you exchanged places? Also, try to see them in a different light, not as father, mother, sister, or friend, but as if they are just another you. In this process you and they are one.

- To listen, *obere* in Latin, means "to give as a gift." You should not be in a hurry to listen, but offer the gift of spacious and abundant time. Listening produces nothing except love. Try not to communicate haste. Do not try to talk the other out of their feelings. Cheap comforts are to be checked at the hospital door for they lead to minimizing the other's experiences.

- Be patient with this process, and offer the gift of time This requires passionate presence and compassionate listening.

The root meaning in Latin of the word "compassion" is "to be there with another's passion." The root word for compassion in Hebrew is the same root word as "womb," to provide a place of warmth and safety. The Greek word for "understand" means "to stand under" or "to get close enough to view the wisdom of the other person."

- It does not help to use your own experience as a yardstick of another's experience. Avoid saying things like "I understand your pain." Everyone sees their experiences of pain and pleasure as unique. At the time of death, no one wants to hear that you know what they are going through, for in fact, you don't. You only know that when you cross that bridge someday.

- Sometimes people need the permission to die that comes from hearing, "We will be okay. You have lived a full life. We will miss you, but it is time for you to die." This simple act of permission frees the dying person from feeling guilt about dying.

- You can coach the person in their breathing, even at the moment of death. Much as you did when your wife was in childbirth and you coached her in Lamaze breathing, you can breathe with the dying person. With each fleeting breath, they are moving into death.

- Remember that dying does not mean "useless." The dying person can learn from those around him or her. Even more so, you can learn from the dying person. Think of this person as a "death scout," someone sent out ahead of you to give you a sense of what death may be like when it's your turn.

Conclusion

In 2001 I had the opportunity to serve at Mother Teresa's home for orphans and dying children in Haiti. I never thought I could be with a child as he or she died. The strength to do so came from a source outside of myself. On several occasions, I was in the presence of infants when they died. Because my English words had no meaning to the Creole-speaking children, the silent acts of love carried these infants to their death.

A lovely child, Sonya, had the brightest, biggest eyes. Her pencil-thin arms and legs did not detract from the wonderful spark in her eyes. She was about a year old. I fed Sonya, changed her diaper, and comforted her in her pain from malnutrition. As I prepared to leave Haiti, I held Sonya one last time. I laid her down in her crib and said good-bye as she gently died. I was grief stricken. As I expressed my pain to the head sister in the home, she said, "Thank you for the love you showed the children, especially to Sonya. She died knowing someone loved her."

Dying is your greatest challenge in life as well as your greatest spiritual opportunity. Words like "success," which meant so much in the first half, have little value in the dying process. Dying is about accepting your significance in life and the love that has been given to you. By dealing with your dying, you become a teacher to others as well as your own best friend. Embrace death for all that it brings you.

Chapter 9

Living in the In-Between

Life's second half is about making sense of changes and how you view and adapt to these changes. In the second half, changes seem more complex and momentous. It feels like you've moved into a new house, arranged the furniture, gotten comfortable, and then someone knocks on your door and tells you it's time to move out. This is the nature of change.

The Changes of the Second Half of Life

Life's first half is mostly about beginnings. The second-half journey means facing the changes that come as simultaneous endings and beginnings. By midlife you have probably faced a number of endings: the empty nest, a lost job, illness, a lost marriage, the death of parents, or the loss of other relationships. You may have faced several beginnings: a geographic move, a new job or career, going back to school to learn a new trade, early retirement, grandparenting, overcoming addiction and beginning a sober life, or starting a family a second time around.

You may have initiated these endings and beginnings, such as breaking a long-term relationship, requesting a job transfer, starting an exercise program, or losing weight. You may have anticipated some of these changes, although you may not have understood the impact of the changes until they occurred, such as a child leaving for college or joining the military, early retirement, the death of aging parents, or turning fifty. Some changes may have been forced on you, such as getting laid off from work. You may have had to deal with the disability of a loved one as a result of an accident. Unexpected changes can significantly affect your life, such as having a heart attack at fifty. Some of these changes may be viewed as bad, some as good. It all depends on how you view the impact of change.

Brett was sixty. His children from his first marriage were fully grown. He was a grandfather. When a major hurricane hit his home city of Charleston, South Carolina, Brett and his second (and significantly younger) wife were homebound for a week without electricity and without anything to do. Nine months later he became a father again at the age of sixty-one.

Bob was a successful businessman who was fortunate to retire at fifty-eight. He and his wife had great plans for how they would spend their years in retirement: cruises, touring the world, spending time visiting their adult children. Then his wife had a stroke, paralyzing her on one side and placing her in a wheelchair for the rest of her life. Their plans for enjoying his retirement were drastically changed.

Barry was fifty when he decided he had enough of a thirty-year-long unhappy marriage. He announced to his wife and college-age children that he was getting a divorce. He had met a woman who brought him to life again. Much to everyone's surprise and anger, Barry followed through on this sudden ending of his marriage and married a much younger woman. Now, years later, he is a totally new man with renewed vigor, enthusiasm for life, and a perpetual smile.

Steve was forty-five when the company he started fell upon difficult financial times. He sold the company, providing him some financial resources but certainly not sufficient to live on for the rest of his life. About that time his teenage daughter contracted Lyme disease and other major health problems. At fifty Steve reassessed all he had achieved and instead of continuing the journey of ascent, he dedicated himself to starting a house for recovering addicts. He now spends most of his waking hours managing the halfway house. This radical shift in priorities likely would not have happened had Steve not entered a time of soul-searching and pain.

Answer these questions in your journal:

☒ What changes have you faced so far in your life? Which of these changes were self-imposed? Which changes were unexpected, sudden, unplanned?

☒ What did it feel like to go through a self-imposed change versus an unplanned change? Which was more difficult for you?

First Come Endings

Before you can understand the process of change you must face what has ended in your life. Endings seem to abound. But endings must come before something new can be born. Before you can become a different person in the second half, you need to let go of the old you and your past life. In endings, you realize something has been lost, but it isn't usually the process of ending that you fear. Why do we cling to what was or what should be ending for us? Tilopa, a tenth-century yogi, said, "It is not the outer objects that entangle us. It is the inner clinging that entangles us" (Rinpoche 1993, 224). We need to let go of what is, so something new can be born.

The first step in dealing with endings is to realize what you are losing. How much of this loss and change is real and how much is in your imagination? You may have had a lot of problems in your life; some of them actually happened. So much of what you envision as changing is in your mind. A job change may feel like looming financial disaster. When a friend dies you may fear the ending of your life, despite all the signs of your good health. Is the ending as bad as you think it will be?

Second, what other changes will occur as a result of this one ending? What is ending for others as well as for you? Michael decided he needed to end a thirty-year career as an engineer and work out of the house as a technician, repairing worn-out small equipment. This decision brought major changes in the family. He was home more. His wife felt less independent because of his increased presence in the house. His teenage children were accustomed to their dad being away from home for business and did not know how to adjust with him around more. The financial impact on the family was significant, since he took a pay cut to do what he loved to do. He was much more contented, but the family was not too sure what to do with these changes.

Tom was an insurance broker with twenty years of business experience. He was bored to death in his work, so at age fifty he decided to open a model train store, something he always wanted to do. There was financial risk to the family. It also meant that Tom's wife and teenage children needed to work in the store sometimes. It also meant making model railroading the centerpiece of their lives as is required in any new business venture.

When you decide to end something, do not be surprised by the reactions of others who think that you have lost your mind. Your action may bring a strong reaction in others as they wonder about the impact of your decision on their lives. They may ask themselves "Am I next? If he wants to end that relationship, he might want to leave the family." Some may feel threatened because you are no longer holding down your accustomed place in their world. It is important to acknowledge the ending with a sympathetic ear to the effects of your decision on others and to inform people in your life about what is changing and why.

Third, you need to disengage from the past, gently. What from the past do you need or want to take with you into the future? What bridges do you not want to burn as something ends? With disengagement needs to come disidentification, when you accept that what is past is no longer part of your life. The disidentification process is really the inner side of the disengagement process. This is often particularly distressing in work transitions, where the old roles and titles were an important aspect of your identity. The impact of this disidentification can be much greater than one imagines in advance—no longer the husband, no longer the boss, no longer living in this house. To bring about an ending, you need to loosen the bonds of who you thought you were, so you can go through the transition to a new identity.

Fourth, you need to go through the process of disenchantment with the old, realizing that some of the significant parts of your old reality were in your head. This is the persona you made for yourself, but it does not fully define you. You are more than the sum of your job description, your titles, and the roles you assumed.

Fifth, an ending is a form of dying. You might feel disoriented, disillusioned, and alone. You may be unsure where you are and where you are going, or you might feel you are without goals. Your loss of power and direction can be frightening, for it threatens the essential qualities of who you thought you were. The key through these stages is to go gently into the change process, to accept the natural flow of change with all of its attendant feelings. Remember that there are no spiritual emergencies in the change process.

Finally, it is helpful to mark the ending with celebrations, to create activities that dramatize the ending, giving you and others a chance to treat the past with respect. It is important to allow yourself and others to take a piece of the old with you. Remember the past; honor it. Yesterday's endings launch tomorrow's significance. It is also true that if you're running away from the past defensively, seeking to obliterate it, you won't get to the future you want.

In your journal, answer these questions about the endings you have experienced:

☒ What has ended in your life? How have you dealt with these endings? Which of these endings have been most painful, difficult, or joyous for you?

☒ Did you denigrate the past or did you honor what was with reverence and respect?

☒ Have you given yourself and others a piece of the past to carry forward into the future?

☒ What is ending for you at this time? What you are likely to lose?

☒ What will this ending mean to others in your life? Are you permitting yourself and others to grieve and express a sense of loss? What are you telling people about what is changing? What is over and what isn't? How are you marking the ending?

What needs to end for you at this time? What needs to end may be the thing you are holding that you do not want to let go. You resist letting go because it feels familiar and safe, although what you are doing may be toxic to you in the long run.

Answer the following questions in your journal:

☒ What are you forcing yourself to do that you don't want to do but should do? What are you doing today solely to please someone else: your spouse, the kids, the boss, friends, family members, and the community? How much of this is just to keep up appearances, to meet someone else's expectations?

☒ What do you maintain that you no longer believe in or feel unsatisfied with? What part of your life is without passion, color, or excitement? What needs to end?

☒ What gets in your way of ending this? What do you need to do to bring it to a close?

The Second Half Is about In-Between Times

In life's second half you face many endings and beginnings, but the second half is mainly about living in the in-between times, between endings and beginnings. The essential question is how you will live in the times between endings and beginnings. How will you pass through peaceful endings into passionate beginnings, through that painful, neutral zone of life?

The neutral zone is time in the wilderness, life's desert places. In the first half, it seemed like there was plenty of time left on the clock, that you were just in the first or second quarter of the game. The in-between times seemed to pass more quickly, if they came at all. In the first half, you sought but rarely found answers to your questions. In the second half, it may feel like you are running a two-minute offense without the luxury of time-outs. Also, you may not feel as resilient in the second half, that you are playing the game with less bench strength and energy to get you through. Some of your usual players have been sidelined by injuries. By the second half, most of the first-half answers you found no longer work. In the in-between times of the second half, the questions seem to be more significant and the answers more illusory.

What are some of the in-between times in the second half? Your career may be ending, but you are still not quite sure what you will do now. You may know your marriage is over or you may be in the process of separating from the family, but there is nothing yet to take the place of the love you once felt in your heart. Your physical strength may have lessened, but your wisdom strength has not yet become apparent. You may know the belief systems you had in the first half do not work for you any longer, but you do not, as yet, have any others to replace them. The old answers no longer work, and all you are left with are the questions.

When faced with the times between endings and beginnings, the tendency is to want to move quickly through the neutral zone and on to something new. The problem is that you feel immobilized by the lack of answers, so you linger in the past. It is not that you love the past and want to cling to what has been, although that may be the case. It is more that you fear the uncertainties as to what lies ahead. Living without answers creates anxiety. It is life on a trapeze when there does not appear to be any rope to hold onto and not much of a safety net below you. During the in-between, your motivation may decline. Old weaknesses, long patched over or compensated for, reemerge. It may be a time of error and wild fanaticism as you swing on the trapeze, grasping at anything you can hold. The old is dying or has died, and the new has not yet been born. You must allow the past to drift away, for a beginning is only as great as the endings that preceded it and the time of reflection you spend in between. In fact, life is really a series of endings, in-betweens, and beginnings, all interconnected.

Endings breed new life just as much as the order of life in the first half bred habit. You cannot push this process of chaos along any faster than it wants to go. Even as it takes nine months to have a baby no matter how many doctors you put on the job, so too it takes time in the wilderness of change. It is like Moses' wilderness. It took forty years not because they were lost, but because that is the period of a generation. It took a short time for Moses to get the people out of Egypt but forty years to get Egypt out of the people.

What we call "confusion" during our wilderness time may be just something we don't understand yet. You expect life to be a straight line from the old to the new, but the path does not go that way. It is a meandering country lane, instead of a four-lane highway, through change in the second half, with overlapping roadways, most of which you initially cannot see.

In this time of wandering, you want answers, but often there are none. What are you to do? In these times, you may feel lost. The neutral zone is a lonely place. You may feel like you must make the most of the situation and get out of the in-between time as fast as possible. The wilderness is just like building a fire: at first it's smoky and your eyes water, but later you get the desired result. Thus you need to light the fire within you with tears and effort, to see this time as not only the absence of something, but as the transition between two phases of life.

In your journal, answer these questions:

☒ What were the in-between times of your life? What have you felt during these times? Describe the confusion and sense of loss you felt during these in-between times.

☒ What did you do in these times? Did you rush to fill the void with other activities?

How to Turn the Scary into the Sacred In-Between

Although you may not like to live in a state where there are more questions than answers, you need to live in between endings and beginnings. This is to stand between the polarity of two opposites, between what was and what is yet to be, holding together the opposites.

The key in the second half is to turn the scary in-between times into sacred in-between times. What makes something sacred? The sacred is the movement toward deeper truth, deeper connection, deeper understanding. Whatever helps us move in that direction is sacred. Here are some steps to get through the scary aspects of the neutral zone and convert them into sacred times.

Step 1: You need not be defensive about the apparent unproductive time-out. Despite our work-oriented culture, wherein if you are not productive, you are useless, in-between time is actually a moratorium from your conventional mode of living, an extended time-out. In the apparent aimless activity of your time, important spiritual work is happening, although it may not be evident to you at the time. Give it time to grow organically. Allow yourself the apparent downtime to gaze at the moon, walk gently on the earth, discover the awe of the night, or dream.

Step 2: An important activity in the neutral zone is to surrender to what is outside your control. This is not easy. Let go of your attempts to gain control of your world. The control you once thought you had is illusory. You really never were in control, although you thought you were. Allow the process to take you where you may not want to go, for you can only dare to enter what you let go of. Do not worry if the messages you receive do not make any sense. There is nothing logical about the in-between. Your spirit does not work from logic.

Step 3: Find a regular time and place to be alone. When you are in transition, you need to have quiet time with your innermost thoughts. Put a "do not disturb" sign on your life for a time. These alone times can be found when jogging, sitting in your car without the radio on, or on a spiritual retreat providing you the solitude and silence you desperately need yet greatly fear. You need to see the world through soft eyes, the eyes that view the heavens at night. You need to listen attentively to the stirrings of life and hope within you.

Step 4: Keep a journal of your thoughts, dreams, conversations, and feelings. When you are lost, you may not see the important signs along the way that can lead you out of the forest. This is not a trivial kind of diary keeping like you did as a teenager. Give yourself time to reflect on what is really going on for you; your reflections and the serendipitous events in your life may give you guidance.

Step 5: Whereas time alone is important, in the in-between times, you also need to occasionally be there with others who can share the process with you. It is a time when communication and relationships are essential. It is a time to not be alone, although outwardly it seems as if no one else can understand what you are going through. With whom in your life can you share your current confusion? To what extent does your partner know what you are going through during the in-between times? How much of your disorientation have you shared with others?

Step 6: When all around you seems to be changing, you need to identify the continuities in your life. What has not changed? What is there to hold onto in your life? What do you need to change? What do you need to leave alone for now? List the things that have not changed in your life. What are the roots that tie you to the continuities in your life, such as the house you grew up in? Add these to your list of continuities. What have you set aside that served as continuities before, such as your old interests, hobbies, earlier relationships, or former recreation, that you'd like back in your life? What do you not want to lose or see end?

Step 7: Although you may not like to be in the dark, you need to wrestle with the paradoxes of life, the mystery of the questions. Only then can you find light. Nothing makes the light stand out as well as darkness. When you surrender to the darkness, you become more aware of the subtle sounds, the sensations, and the movements in your life. You experience more. It is the very darkness that you are trying to avoid that allows you to see the sparks of transformation.

Step 8: To add light to the darkness, you need to turn things upside down. That means to discover gratitude in the darkness, joy in sadness, and life in the ruins of your life. We discover new life not only in new landscapes but through new eyes. New eyes that come after darkness force you to find new vision, seeing your life from a fresh perspective. This may mean cleaning your space through a change in attitude.

Step 9: To move you through the in-between times, it may be helpful to create a bit of discord in your daily routine to see what should change. Even in the in-between times, you can become complacent and slow to move out of the neutral zone. It may be easier to coast too long in neutral. To stop coasting, try doing the following:

- Take a different route to work. Spend your lunch in a totally new way. Move your desk. Take a three-minute break every hour. Every day look for a chance to say to yourself "Why not?"

- Force yourself to plan to do something this weekend that you have never done before. Every day force yourself to say no to three requests.

- Volunteer to do something you normally wouldn't agree to do. Ask someone that question you have always wanted to ask them.

You may do all of these things, yet sometimes in the darkness nothing happens. If you find yourself in the in-between times and nothing happens, what do you do then? Perhaps you have tried to add light too quickly. You know what happens when you move quickly from darkness to light. You are blinded by the light and unable to see what is right in front of you. You may need to live in the darkness a little longer, allowing your eyes to refocus. You may be so entrenched in the old way of looking at your life that you cannot surrender to the answers coming from an angle entirely different from where you were looking.

Also, when darkness persists, you may need to follow your own instincts. Your true self may be asking you to stop rehashing old issues and to go after live opportunities. Perhaps your instincts are telling you it is time to take action and to pursue your goals with a new focus. There may be indicators of the way out of the neutral zone: the chance meetings with people you have not seen in a long time, meeting someone who changes your vision. Other people can be mirrors for you, reflecting the light you need to find your way out of the darkness. Pay attention to those chance happenings, the serendipities of change. Carl Jung called this "synchronicity." Other indicators may be a mystical experience in which you see, hear, or feel something you have never experienced before or a dream that says, "Time to move on." Perhaps it is an emerging opportunity that is in alignment with your new insights. Pay attention to them! The worst thing you can do in the darkness is to avoid the insights staring you in the face, to keep doing what you have always done. To do so is to avoid the light that is bringing you out of your darkness.

Answer these questions in your journal:

☒ What chance occurrences have happened in your life recently that you barely noticed but may be calling you to do something different? What role do these chance events play in your life? How are you being led to respond?

☒ Do these chance happenings trigger anything from your past? What are you not seeing? Is there a pattern here? What options are there that you do not yet see?

Your Age and How to Move through the In-Between Times

Regardless of your age, there are concerns you might ponder in the in-between times, such as your search for life's deeper meaning or how to better manage finances to insure adequate future income. Your concern might be seeking a rootedness in your past, your ethnic group, or lost friendships, or how to be more involved in social, peace, and justice issues. You might seeks ways to simplify your life or to lead an environmentally responsible lifestyle.

Most importantly, regardless of your age, when you are in the in-between times, you need to ask yourself what are you saving time for? How might the future look different for you? What are the potential doors waiting to open? Do you believe that you are not alone, that you will be cared for? Are you ready to move on and to accept the consequences of what you are choosing—consequences for both others and yourself? Are you ready to move out of the in-between times?

Your response to the in-between times will be shaped by how old you are. It is through the lens of age that we view the future. As we age, the viewfinder seems to project a shorter image on the screen as there may be less time left on the clock for you to enact your dreams and realize your insights. If you are in your forties and fifties, you might find your way through the neutral zone by reevaluating your career or occupation and reassessing your financial goals, lifestyle, priorities, and values. It may be a time to relate differently to your teenage children or to your aging parents and to reassess your relationship with your partner. Perhaps you need to become more deeply involved in your friendships. Maybe this is a time for you to take a new interest in fitness or rediscovering a relationship with nature.

If you are in your sixties, you may need to make a career change into a new form of work or expand your avocational and volunteer interests. You may need to adjust to more constant companionship with a partner or to single life, or face the death of friends. In your sixties, you may need to reap the rewards from the work you have done and focus on what is vital and right for you. You may need to seek and enjoy mentoring opportunities with young people and to cultivate new relationships. Finally, the sixties are a time to enjoy the rewards of a spiritual quest.

If you are in your seventies or older, you may seek to pass on wisdom from your life experiences to those younger than you. This is a time to accept the naturalness of death and prepare for the mystery of what comes next, to put your affairs in order by making suitable living arrangements for your later days. These are the years when you can find nature a solace and kindly speak the truth as you see and understand it by embracing and enjoying spiritual maturity.

Facing New Beginnings

To face new beginnings it helps to frame your life in a way different from the first half, which was marked by an emphasis on success and achievement. It is important not to focus on power, prestige, and possessions. Beginnings in the second half are not journeys of ascent where you continue to press your marriage, job, finances, and health to the limit.

Beginnings also happen for men who have not known achievement, recognition, and prosperity, who might say, "Why am I doing this anyway, when it isn't what I really want to do and I haven't made money at it either?" Many have had the desire for ascent frustrated in the first half and bring unfinished business to the second half even as they seek deeper meaning. They may see the two as being interlinked. If you didn't achieve much outward success because you weren't inspired by what you were doing, and even may have fought it, you might succeed in spite of yourself by doing something you love. Having failed by being inauthentic, by doing things just to please others, you might succeed by being authentic. You might ascend unintentionally and effortlessly on the wings of your inspiration. That can also be part of the magic of the transition and the new beginning.

Ironically, after waiting in the in-between time for a new beginning, when the desired beginning comes, you may be afraid of it. Beginnings reactivate old anxieties and establish once and for all that something has ended. A beginning may also be a gamble. It may feel easier to stay in your youthful enthusiasm and the security of first-half struggles. In the first half you might have done work that was forced on you by family pressures, a lack of other options, or because that was what you "had" to do to support your family. But in the first half, at least you knew the rules. Perhaps your new idea will not work out. Others may think your ideas are crazy, unrealistic, or odd. You may look at the road ahead and wonder if this is the right path to take.

Rarely is the path into new beginnings well marked. Unless you are struck by divine revelation, you may wonder if this is what you ought to do. You want assurances that this is the right thing for you, to know the path of what's ahead. The truth is, the path ahead is often uncertain. In youth, things seemed more clearly marked. In the second half, the path is often an adventure into the unknown. Theologian Thomas Merton, when asked what was the path in life, described it as if you are standing in front of a field of freshly fallen snow and wanted to know where the path is. You have to cross the field. Then there is a clearly marked path (Merton 1956).

To face beginnings, it is important not to fear them. Life in the second half is an adventure of continuous change. Change in the second half is a movement to authenticity; it is an invitation to connect to your deepest self, to other people, to nature, and to life itself. Second-half change involves digging deeper versus growing upward simply for the status that it brings. If life is seen as an adventure of continuous change, you see beginnings in a larger context, as a natural process that takes time and requires an equal measure of faith and perseverance along the way. Such a vantage point will help you move into beginnings more gracefully. You will have a broader range of options in living with beginnings, and you can reach new planes of awareness more easily than if you resist the perils of beginnings.

Answer these questions in your journal to assess your state of readiness for beginnings:

☒ Can you face change with your eyes open? Do you want to learn more about yourself, to see life as an adventure of continuous change?

☒ How ready are you to take action to implement your plans or ideas? Do you know what you want to do next? What are the steps you need to take to move into a new beginning?

☒ How secure do you feel about what you have accomplished in life? Do you feel valued? If so, you may be ready to move into a new beginning.

In other chapters, I wrote about a minister friend who decided in his early fifties to try his hand at songwriting. After years as a minister, he gave up his occupation to devote more time to writing music. At first he was overwhelmed by the usual feelings of anxiety: "How will I pay the bills? Am I nuts giving up a secure career to try writing musicals and songs?" He accepted a position as a part-time interim pastor and spent his remaining time writing music. Within a year, his calendar was booked with several musical opportunities. Two years later, the fears still occasionally surface, but the more frequent problem is keeping focus on why he made the change in the first place. He has been amazed at how many new paths he can take. At each turn in the road, he must discern if this is a beginning or a dead end. Watching this process unfold is exciting, frightening, and life giving.

Tom retired from the navy, at fifty, after a career as a naval officer. After ten years working in the corporate sector and floundering in a bad marriage, at sixty he moved to New Zealand to manage health care programs with his new wife. Talk about stepping forward into a new beginning! He is happier than ever on his farm in the mountains of New Zealand.

Bob had a successful career as a contractor, was in a satisfying marriage, lived a quiet life on a lake in Vermont, and was comfortable in his lifestyle. At forty-five, Bob and his wife decided it was time for a beginning, and they adopted a child. Rather than miss out on fatherhood while working long hours as a contractor, Bob decided to go to law school via correspondence. His wife continued her career as a teacher and became the primary breadwinner while Bob stayed at home with their adopted son, Peter. Bob passed the bar exam and now practices law from his house in between changing diapers and Peter's nap times. Bob left the comfort zone, ended a successful career, and ventured into the unknown of a new beginning as a stay-at-home dad and attorney.

Exercise: Making Choices

The following exercise summarizes the steps on page 124 and will help you move from endings through the neutral zone to beginnings. The exercise will help you understand the language of choice and learn to let go as well as learn to live in the in-between time.

1. Be aware of your growing discomfort with what is happening or has happened in your life. Where do you feel anxious, depressed, worried, isolated, and alone? Often your discontent is the best view of the areas where your foundations are shifting. An important part of this awareness may be facing your avoidance of reality, facing denial and repression, which keeps you locked in neutral.

2. Begin to realize the need to change, to choose another lifestyle. What keeps you from doing things differently?

3. Checking out available options is an important step. I always counseled employees to check the help-wanted section of the newspaper just to know what their options were. Become informed about the possibilities available to you. Too often you may see yourself at a dead end when in fact there are exit roads all around you.

4. To get out of the in-between time you need to have a sense of what you want. After that, the second question is what are you willing to do to get what you want. What is the cost of change, of getting out of the neutral zone?

5. Now comes the hard part: being aware of where you resist change. As strange as it may sound, being in the neutral zone may feel better than facing the unknown and moving into a new beginning. Sometimes the known, despite how painful that may be, is safer than the shock of the new. Therefore, be aware of what you are holding onto for security.

6. Practice change one step at a time. Do not try to conceive of a totally changed life. That can either pose an unrealistic fantasy world, which will likely never be realized, or it may feel so monumental a change that you become frozen in the present. Do not attempt to envision a new life, a new partner, a new home, a new job, and a new geography all at once. Instead, take small steps forward, practicing moving ahead one day at a time.

These are the steps to move from endings through the neutral zone into new beginnings. Now is the time to get started on your new second-half journey.

Conclusion

Living in the in-between times is exciting and frightening. These are the times when you learn by far the most about yourself and your life. Do not rush through the in-between times. They have much to teach you.

Chapter 10

New Sources of Refreshment: Your Spiritual Life

The second half is essentially a spiritual journey. There are two major spiritual tasks you face in the second half: discovering what you are to be from now on and moving into a deeper inner life with a new sense of your world and yourself. It is as simple (and complex) as that. The second-half journey seeks to grow in grace and not in doing more.

Second-half spirituality involves the deepest dimension of who you were made to be. It gives you meaning in living by addressing questions of self-worth. It reveals that life's ultimate meaning cannot lie in speed, consumerism, achievement, and physical beauty as defined by your culture. Like the headlight of a train moving swiftly through the night, the later years throw light on the turns and landscapes that lie ahead, preparing you for each passage. Finally, second-half spirituality enables the next generation to see in you the fullness of life. If young people see in you despair and depression, they will cling to their youth as long as time allows.

The Spiritual Journey: Downward

Paul is eighty-two years old and describes himself as a religious mutt, raised Catholic, practicing Buddhism and Chinese qigong, and working in an ecumenical organization. He oozes warmth, compassion, and wonder in all he does. Yet, he confesses that his personal journey has not been easy. He has dealt with the demons of workaholism, alcoholism, and his physical infirmities. Sober now for thirty years, Paul confesses that he has been to his own personal hell and back. Paul will also tell you that without this downward journey he perhaps never would have found his true self, his essential, spiritual nature.

Men recoil from the idea of going downward. We have "descentaphobia." We fear we will be insignificant when removed from the power, possessions, and prestige that were the driving forces in life's first half. In the twentieth century, men sought a number of ways of dealing with this fear of insignificance, such as the Promise Keepers and the Million Man March. They point to a traditional way of dealing with power through a continued journey of ascent, going upward and outward.

Gary, forty-six, says, "When I was in my late thirties, I was on top of the world. I graduated from Princeton and had an MBA from Harvard, a six-figure salary, a spacious home, beautiful wife, bright children, and more possessions than I ever wanted. When Promise Keepers came to our church, I signed up. I wanted to be head of my household too. I was on top of everything else; why not the family as well? Now I am in my late forties. My kids are leaving for college, my wife has her own career, and I am at the summit of my career. In my first half, I went upward. Now I need to find who I truly am, not what others say I should be."

Matt is a fifty-five-year-old African American. His first half was not the typical affluent white male journey of ascent. He fought for all of his success in life. Yet he still wanted to be somebody. When the Million Man March happened, he went to Washington, D.C., and claimed for the first time his birthright as a man. Five years later, he sees that the march gave him a new sense of pride and value. He now feels he needs help through his inner journey. He must now retain the gains of the march while looking inward to see his pain and wounds.

Second-half spirituality is primarily a journey of limitation, realizing you cannot have it all. It is seeing the limits of your power and the language of your pain. The journey takes you through pain to trust. By midlife you have experienced some pain through wounds in relationships, career setbacks, illness, and death of friends. What you do with that pain largely sets the tone for how you will live in the second half.

Answer these questions in your journal:

☒ What emotional or physical pain have you had or do you still have? How have you transformed your pain?

☒ How do you transmit your pain to others or yourself?

Downward into the Desert

Digging deeper requires alone time in the desert with periods of feeling lost. Men don't like to be lost; after all, we never ask for directions. Be careful of the man who tells you life is one joy after another with no desert times. He is fooling himself. Spirituality involves time in the darkness, where you are reborn into something new. The first noble truth of Buddhism is life is suffering. Jesus said you must take up your cross and bear it (Mark 8:34). This is a basic truth of life—eventually, all of us must travel the desert journey.

There are few images as powerful as the desert, filled with awe, terror, and exquisite color. From Canyon de Chelly to the red rocks of Sedona, Arizona, from Ayers Rock in Australia, to the sand dunes of eastern California and the stillness of the Sahara desert, the life-blood of the earth seems to have risen to the surface. There you move away from the lush phases of life filled with abundance to a barrenness where there seems to be no life.

There have been times in my life when the physical desert held great sway. In 1985 my family went to Morocco and we drove into the Sahara desert. Alone, with nothing but the wind blowing, devoid of other sounds, there was a stillness, barrenness, and aridness that I had never before experienced. Out of the scorching heat radiating from the ground came a sense of fear and awe of my aloneness. In that moment there also was a sense of peace. I've had similar experiences at the monoliths of Monument Valley in southern Utah. As I walked through the valley of Canyon de Chelly I felt alone, yet life abounded everywhere. The colors of the rock walls lightened an otherwise arid and dark place. I knew these landscapes described the middle part of my life. Their mythic contours, these places of abandonment, fraught with Sinai images and spiritual dryness, touched me at my deepest level. Geographer Ellen Churchill Semple states that humans are "a product of the earth's surface. Ideas take on a certain gigantic simplicity" (Semple 1911, 1).

If you live in an urban area, you may have few opportunities to experience a rugged terrain. Instead of idealizing the expanses of America's Southwest, the Outback of Australia, or the Sahara desert, which few ever step foot on, you can find it at night in the dark sky of your backyard. You may have to work a little harder to isolate yourself from city noise but you can explore great horizons by simply looking upward into a darkened evening sky. You may find it in the aloneness of your apartment room in the city or in a corporate office.

The desert symbolizes not just a place but also a state of being. Most of your daily life may be filled with blasts of the boring and ordinary. Yet, it is in the deserted center of your day when you feel most alone. It is when you face the ultimate question in life, "Why am I here?"

When you confront a darkened expanse, whether in Africa, your backyard, or your own aloneness, what words are there to describe the experience? You encounter the desert of place and person and you find yourself out of words. Stripped of any images to describe what you see or feel, you stand naked without the protection of language.

Michael tells of his dark night when the company he owned was audited. An accountant reviewed the company books and erroneously concluded that there was fraud; Michael would be charged with the errors and likely sent to jail. For days Michael wandered aimlessly in the prison of his fears only to find out the accountant was wrong. Michael was guilty of no wrongdoing and his anxiety was ill-founded. But the terror of that time did not go away easily. Paradoxically, at that same moment Michael also experienced the indescribable love most apparent when he felt totally lost. Meister Eckhart said, "God whispers to us in our happiness, speaks to us in our everyday lives, but yells to us in our pain and despair" (Eckhart 1996, 11).

Further, the spiritual journey downward is not always a dark, dread-filled experience. It may be a time when things become obscure. You cannot see or grasp what is happening, as in a dark night. Sometimes things are darkened in order to keep us safe—so we know that we don't know and we are more likely then to surrender our will to what might be. Whether tender or tragic, the dark night always involves being taken where you would not go on your own. In the dark times you trust something else to be your guide.

When describing the desert times of life, Plato used the allegory of the cave. Carl Jung spoke about the shadow. Moses met God in the barrenness of Sinai. Jesus after his baptism wandered for forty days in the desert, tempted by power, possessions, and prestige. In the desert, stripped of achievement and power, you lose your old self and what you thought mattered. The goal of the desert is *kenosis*, an emptying of your ego and an opening to something greater than yourself, known only through surrender and aloneness.

In the desert you enter a place of relentless deprivation only to find yourself. Even in the midst of desert totality there is a brilliant darkness where light shines on your soul. That is the moment of clarity when you see the new light of day and say, "Yes, I am going this way."

This does not mean that simply by going into a desert time you will find illumination. You might, you might not. Although the desert experience can exert a powerful tug on your life, it is not an automatic process of transformation unless there is an encounter with the tears of absence. The presence of absence awakens your silence and refreshes your courage with the purity of detachment. Absence comes when you finally realize the spiritual truth that you are not all that important.

You may find that in your youth you worried about what people thought of you. In your twenties you worried endlessly about the impressions you made and how people were evaluating you. Sometime in your fifties, you realize that they hardly ever thought about you at all. As a man you likely have presumed yourself to be the center of everyone's attention when in fact you have been performing for an audience that is not listening. When that hits you, something tells you that you are accepted just as you are. When you are in great pain, often something breaks through the darkness and lets you know that you are accepted just as you are with all your flaws and blemishes.

In 1997 I went on retreat in the Pennsylvania mountains and felt insignificant. I wandered to my cabin under the canopy of the starlit sky. I said to myself, "I just want to be significant somewhere." As surely as I write these words I heard a voice say, "You are significant to me." Illumination came when I felt alone and insignificant. In that moment I accepted the grace offered me. I was given the blessing of significance staring me in the face.

Unfortunately such transformation seldom comes in a form that you welcome, as a gentle invitation to change. Rather, it comes as an assault on your stability, demanding abandonment of what previously gave you a sense of security. When you accept your vulnerability in the desert times, you're offered wholeness. The irony is that you hear the good news of change when you are immersed in the bad news of your normal experience. Spirituality based on brokenness demands rethinking of what it means to be a man. You are not your faults, your body, your being a father, husband, or employee. You are more than these. Yes, you have faults, but they are not you. You have roles in life to play, but they are not you. All of these things are changeable. Yet who you are does not get lost with age, disease, or changing circumstances.

Answer these questions in your journal:

☒ What have you come to believe you are?

☒ How do you fit into the grand scheme of life? Where are you significant?

The answers come when you measure yourself by something other than performance. You will be incessantly restless until you turn your woundedness into health, your deformity into beauty, and your embarrassment into laughter.

In the first half you wrestled over life's temptations. In the second half you wrestle for a blessing, even though the original blessing has already been given you. You are accepted just as you are, but you did not see that in your first half. Even as Jacob in the Hebrew Testament wrestled with the angel until he was granted his blessing, so too do you wrestle with the divine, believing that you have a fighting chance. Paradoxically, when you accept that your heart was vacated in the first half by your journey of ascent and you are now absent of the very thing you longed for, love, then you find that you live perpetually in the wonder of the love that has grabbed you already. This invitation to the spiritual life is a call to the high-risk venture of being loved more fiercely than you ever might have dreamed.

Answer these questions in your journal:

☒ When have you experienced aloneness, desert times? Describe that experience. How did you find your way out of it? Did you gain perspective?

☒ If you have not had times alone in the desert, what do you envision that experience would be like for you? What would you find in the desert?

The Journey of "Joys and Sorrows"

Bob, age forty-nine, said, "I once thought life was one continuous party, filled with great happiness and very few sorrows. Then my sister died of breast cancer at thirty-six, my son was born with a hearing disability, and my wife was in a serious auto accident that has left her in constant pain. I ask myself, 'Is life just one sorrow after another?' I want to find a balance in my life between joys, which still are many, and sorrows, which come in waves."

Different cultures view this mystery of joys and sorrows differently. In the West, using either-or language, we seek infinite joys and deny the reality of sorrow. We may be the first culture in history that believes that the material journey without descent is available to us.

From the beginning, world religions have told us that life is both-and. Christianity tells us that by our wounds we are healed. Buddhism teaches us that life is ten thousand joys and ten thousand sorrows." Taoism speaks of the yin and yang of life, the polarity of opposites. Life is a great mystery, composed of light and dark, summer, winter, spring, and fall. These are the many sides of the mystery. You can't have one without the other.

From another source you find the same concept. In Mitch Albom's *Tuesdays with Morrie* (1997, 40), Morrie said, "Life is always a tension of opposites." When Mitch asked Morrie who wins in that tension, Morrie answered, "Love always wins." All spiritual traditions teach us that through death we find love and life.

Answer these questions in your journal:

- ☒ What have been your joys and sorrows in life? How have they shaped you?

- ☒ Where have you experienced the winning power of love in your life?

Downward Means Letting Go

Spirituality is always about letting go your false sense of independence. As a youth you fought for your independence. To be a man was to be self-sufficient. Yet you really never were fully independent. In life's second half you live in a world that is connected to everything that has lived, lives, and will live. Buddhists call this interdependence. To let go is to acknowledge you are interdependent with others. The more you try to control, the less control you have. And conversely, in the words of poet Wendell Berry, "Seed of song, work or sleep, no matter the need, what we let fall, we keep" (1985, 263).

What control do you still seek to maintain? Do you have the courage to change what you can change? What do you need to let go of today? Do you have the serenity to accept what you cannot change? Do you have the wisdom to know the difference between what you can change and what you cannot? Do you have a sense of interdependence with others?

The Interplay of the Outward and the Inward

The movement inward is what makes the second half exciting. In the first half you sought answers to life's questions by your own effort. In the second half the answers find you. If you are to become the unique individual you are, a new birth needs to happen within you, perhaps a rebirth of elements dormant for some time. What is being born in you is the harvesting of satisfaction, excitement for life, finding new meaning in everyday existence, and a freedom to pursue your goals while time permits. Just as a pregnant woman yearning for the being forming within her, she must attend to her body, so too as you age there are outward physical, social, and emotional aspects to your journey requiring attention.

Also critical is emotional health, having a sense of well-being, demonstrated in healthy self-esteem and emotional peace. Albert, a fifty-year-old recovering alcoholic, says, "It wasn't until five years into recovery when I finally felt better physically and emotionally, that I was able to understand more fully the spiritual aspects of my inner journey toward wellness."

Circumstances in life, though, can present outward barriers to your inward journey. Health problems and an inability to be as physically active as before, external stress from decreased income, sickness among family members, deaths of friends, and insults to self-esteem through downsizing add up to aspects of life beyond your control.

Steve said, "I thought I was doing fine spiritually until my best friend from college, Robert, died at fifty of a heart attack. I became cynical and resentful of people with their seemingly easy lives. I was angry with God. How could God allow my friend to die so young, leaving behind a wife and three children? It was not until I fully grieved my friend's death that I was able to begin again my conversations with God. Now I see how the outward event of my friend's death was an essential, albeit painful, part of my spiritual journey."

A Relationship with Something Greater than Yourself

Central to the inward journey is a sense of continuity of life with something greater than yourself. The great spiritual truth is that your life is not just about you. There is a far greater story being played out. Your task in the inward journey is to discover your role in that greater story. In *Siddhartha*, Hermann Hesse wrote after Siddhartha's wounds were healed, "From that hour Siddhartha ceased to fight against his destiny. There shone in his face the serenity of knowledge, of one who is no longer confronted with conflict of desires, who has found salvation, who is in harmony with the stream of events, with the stream of life, full of sympathy and compassion, surrendering himself to the stream, belonging to the unity of all beings" (1951, 136).

Steve, after losing his best friend, Robert, and going through the grief process, finally saw life and death in a larger context. He saw the legacy of Robert left behind in the faces of Robert's children. Steve was then able to see something purposeful beyond his friend's death. Robert did not die but lives on in the three children who now can continue on the path Robert traveled.

Answer these questions in your journal:

☒ Can you recall a particular situation like Steve's in which you experienced the continuity of your life?

☒ To what extent do you have a sense of relatedness to something far greater than yourself? What do you see as your role in the larger story of life that is being told? What is your legacy in this larger story?

Exercise: A Spiritual Inventory

Respond to these statements as honestly as possible. You may experience the following in your daily life. If so, how often? (6 = many times a day, 5 = every day, 4 = most days, 3 = some days, 2 = once in a while, 1 = never or almost never). In an attempt to be as inclusive as possible, when you see the phrase "something greater than myself" understand it to include spirit, higher power, God, streams of events or life, or the unity of all beings. You can read it as the continuity of generations (as in Steve's story), the continuity of the nation, culture, or tradition, the stewardship of the earth, or a sacred obligation to preserve the conditions of life for future generations.

1. I feel a presence of something greater than myself, a connection to all of life.

2. At times I feel a joy that lifts me out of my daily concerns.

3. I find strength and comfort in my faith, my religion, my spiritual life.

4. I feel deep inner peace or harmony at times in my life.

5. I ask for help from that which is greater than myself, in the midst of daily activities.

6. I feel guided in the midst of daily activities.

7. I feel love for me from something greater than myself and through others.

8. The beauty of creation spiritually touches me.

9. I feel thankful and grateful for my blessings.

10. I feel a selfless caring for others.

11. I desire to be closer to and in union with that which is greater than myself.

Scoring

Now, add your ratings. If you have between 55 and 66 points, spirituality is an integral part of your daily life. If you scored between 45 and 54 points, spirituality is important to you and perhaps you can increase your daily practice. If you scored between 35 and 44 points, you might wish to focus more on your spiritual life. If you scored between 25 and 34 points, spirituality is apparently not very important to you. Finally, if you scored below 24 points, this is an area that may need considerable attention in your daily life.

Finding Your Inner Calling

You have within you a sense of calling, destiny, what you were created to be. A classic story of destiny is in James Hillman's *The Soul's Code* about Ella Fitzgerald. At fifteen Ella appeared on stage at the Apollo Theater in Harlem. The announcer said, "Here's Ella Fitzgerald and she will dance for us." Ella strolled on stage and said, "No, I think I will sing" (Hillman 1993, 21). In that moment her destiny emerged. Singing was what she was called to do and she did it so elegantly all her life.

Finding your calling (what defines you) is part of the second-half spiritual journey. Regardless of whether the calling came to you at fifteen as it did for Ella Fitzgerald or later in life, you need to find it. You may have had an elementary sense of calling earlier in your life. But with responsibilities to face, bills to pay, income to earn, and ladders to climb, you took on a role and perhaps lost your sense of calling over time. The first-half journey has a way of doing that, distracting you from your destiny. Whatever voices inside you that have been silent for years, now need to be heard. In the second half you need to find your calling.

Calling emerges from within, a discovery of what you were intended to be. It is the essential core of who you are. It gives you direction and a unifying theme, with which the other aspects of your life, such as job, recreation, and relationships, need to harmonize. It is "the one thing," Curly told Billy Crystal in *City Slickers*, he must seek in life to find happiness.

Exercise: Finding Your Calling

How do you find your calling, especially if it has been buried under heaps of chores and responsibilities over time? One way is to conduct a job interview with yourself:

Step 1: Begin in stillness. Get away from the chatter around you, retreat to aloneness where you can listen to the voice of your soul that says, "Do this. This is what you were meant to be." In the silence you may find your inner voice bubbling up from deep within you.

Step 2: Listen to the yearnings that sneak up on you in subtle ways. Something may grab you and say, "Pay attention to this. This is important."

Step 3: Figure out what this calling will cost you and the people in your life and ask yourself what you and others are willing to pay in time, money, and emotions, to respond to this calling.

My daughter Heather heard her calling watching the movie *Welcome to Sarejevo*, after I returned from doing relief work in Bosnia. In the film, Marisa Tomei played an aid worker in Bosnia during the war. Heather said, "I want to do that." A year later at my graduation from Yale, Maria de la Soudiere of the International Rescue Committee (IRC) was honored. Heather said, "I want to work for that organization." Two years later she worked as an aid worker with refugees in West Africa after working a year for IRC. She had heard the call in the film and at graduation.

As a child of the sixties, I had a sense of calling for peace and justice. Even today, thirty years later, my eyes well up with emotions whenever I hear songs about oppression, war, and hunger. I need to constantly listen to these yearnings about peace and justice issues.

Where is the calling given to you? Are you paying attention? Be prepared to enter the dark night, which can be overly self-critical with thoughts such as, "You never became the executive you set out to be. You're not very successful after all." Self-doubts from the first half can emerge when you try to find your calling. Allow these doubts to be there. But you do not have to respond to them.

In 1997 I fulfilled a dream of spending a weekend singing songs with Pete Seeger, the folksinger. Others at the retreat had stayed in the peace movement and continued to work for justice since the sixties, which I had not. My shadow kept saying to me, "You let down your dreams of peace. Look at these people who kept their eye on the prize. Aren't you ashamed of yourself?" I awakened the next day with the realization that I did not have to respond to this self-criticism and I still had time to do something about these yearnings.

Facing Our Calling with Humility

Dare to fail. "If you don't make mistakes, you aren't really trying" (Ventura 1990, 145). Mistakes are how you move past your old limits into a new calling. Learn to laugh at your mistakes. Life is filled with one humiliation after another. Get over it! Don't discard your calling because you didn't get it right the first time around.

In his younger days, Bill Moyers, the journalist, enrolled in seminary and was ordained as a Baptist minister. Years later, after leaving the ministry and spending more than a quarter century in politics and the media, he said, "I thought it was a call to the ministry. But it turned out to be a wrong number" (1989, 145).

Realize that by responding to your calling you are not just switching careers. You are redefining your essence, crossing the threshold, digging deeper, into a new dimension of yourself. What you once thought defined you no longer does.

Listening and decoding your calling requires intuition. It must be renewed and deepened throughout your life. You need to listen amid the fray of life to the voices of intuition and decide more consciously what part they will play in the second half.

Remember, the true test of a calling is not found in work, money, or success. Work can give you many things, but it can never teach you how to sing. Money measures what the bank can hold. Calling measures what your heart can hold. Success isn't everything, wholeness is.

Now answer these questions in your journal:

- ☒ What gives you a sense of wholeness in life? That likely is your calling.

- ☒ What parts of you went underdeveloped in the first half? What would be incomplete in your life if you never did this one thing?

☒ What is still waiting to be born in you? What are you called to now?

Finding Your Values

The essence of the second-half journey is finding values that encompass simplicity and acceptance of what is. Values may mean deciding what you are going to do with what you have accumulated and letting go what you don't need, giving up material things that no longer matter. Finding new values means you need to find new reasons for living.

The consequences of genes, gender, race, class, marital status, income, alcohol and drug abuse, cigarette smoking, and preventive health care all pile up. Genes and lifestyle may be significant determinants of your health status and longevity up to the age of sixty or sixty-five (Sheehy 1998). After that, if you escaped catastrophic illnesses during the critical middle-life period from forty-five to sixty-five, it is your core values that will most likely determine the quality and duration of your life. Successful aging is actually a values choice. New values in the second half give you a new viewfinder to see the breathtaking panorama of your life. With new values you get a 360-degree view in all directions.

Erik Erikson, in his eighties, wrote in *Vital Involvement in Old Age*, "The life cycle does more than extend itself into the next generation. It curves back on the life of the individual, allowing a re-experiencing of earlier stages in a new form" (1986, 87). This new values-driven path is still largely unmarked. Most men don't even know it exists.

To aid in finding new values in the second half, answer these questions in your journal:

☒ How have you moved from the first-half value of competing to the second-half value of connecting? Connecting means being open to both giving and receiving from the heart and not just from the head.

☒ What do you value now? What barriers interfere with the expression of that?

☒ How have you maintained an open, loving heart in the presence of evil, suffering, violence, and hatred in the world? What might help you manifest more love in the world?

☒ How would your life be structured to accommodate your commitment to live out your new values?

Claiming Your Inner Story

Without memory there is no hope, and your memory is found in your life story. By claiming your story, warts and all, you affirm the value of your life. Claiming your story, with its celebrations and crises, brings a sense of identity to your second half. Bob said, "Everything I have done in my career has trained me to perform my work today."

Both the fear of forgetting and the need to remember mark the second half. Your memory is more than a resource for efficient living or a reservoir of colorful and entertaining stories. Beneath the annoyance you feel at not being able to recall names and dates or find your glasses is the nagging fear that some part of you is slipping away. What you are feeling is that by losing things you fear you will lose what defines your identity.

Remembering events and people from your past lets you claim and share yourself with others. Somewhere within you still lives the boy racing across the grass in the summer sunshine, the kid finding his way in his first friendships, the teen on his first date. You do not just have old memories, you are those memories. They are you and memories retrace your journey. The Hebrew Scriptures speak of aging as being "full of days," which captures the deepest meaning of remembering. Events that are finished live on in your existence, even though you may not be able to remember all of the details of these events. They are essential to your being; they have entered into your life's fabric. The past is not slipping away and distancing itself from you. It is piling up and is an untapped reservoir of comfort.

More so than simply living in the past, or nostalgia for the good old days, reclaiming your story brings the past into the present in such a way that it influences present decisions and conduct. Open the album of your life, find scenes in which you felt loved, where you were joyful. It may be a wedding day, the birth of a child, family holiday times, a birthday celebration with friends. Look at that feeling and hold it close. The work of memory is not simply recalling old dates, names, and places. It is the reawakening of the moments that brought healing.

Memory allows you to see that everything that ever was continues to be. Something of the richness of your life continues to touch you through the people you loved and who loved you as well as the people you taught and who taught you. Some memories may be painful. How you view past memories affects how you live in the present. Regret, hurt, and guilt from the past contribute to the bitterness you may feel. Denial of pain can sap your energy. Reclaiming your story allows you finally to transform your pain and no longer transmit it.

Exercise: Reclaiming Your Story

Step 1: Pass your stories on as gifts to family, in scrapbooks or old letters and by visiting childhood sites. Take your children to the home where you were raised as an important transition and continuity for them and for you. You may find it difficult to recall details like names and dates. Your memory can be awakened through "recalling tags," events that profoundly affected you. These events reveal the joyous mysteries of your life.

Step 2: Find ways of triggering memories through symbols that gave you meaning. For example, my dad gave me his caddie badge he had as a boy. That symbol told me a great deal about his youth and what he treasured. Share these symbols with the next generation. It is a way of saying, "This is who I am," and not "This is who I was." You are all of these experiences.

Step 3: Sit down with a tape recorder and tell stories of your childhood and youth. Let your family ask questions. Explore side roads that may not be clearly marked in your memory. Tell the stories in a way that offers the design of your life, the shape that makes each life experience unique and gives it meaning. This pattern, relating part to part and part to whole, gives significance to otherwise meaningless experiences, piecing together a unified self from the fragments of your life. It helps others say, "Oh, that's why you are as you are. Now I understand you better."

Number Your Days: Having a Sense of Wonder and Gratitude

Spirituality is grounded in the capacity to number your days, which begins with a sense of wonder, an ability to live in the present moment. Aging is a time to sort out the more important from the less important things in life. As this happens the elemental realities of life assume greater significance, such as children and grandchildren, nature, plants, physical and emotional contact, textures, colors, shapes. Wonder is the prelude to gratitude. You notice for the first time a hummingbird flitting about or the first robin of spring. You catch the beauty in the face of a friend and hear the laughter of a child. You take a walk as a form of giving thanks. It is time you took a loving look at the realities of your life.

Exercise: The Greatest Gifts in Your Life

Here are some ways to explore and celebrate your memories and your life. These exercises can help you discover the greatest gifts life has brought you.

- List the things that gave you the greatest joys in life. Focus on the people and joyful events in each period of your life. List the times you felt awe and the circumstances that brought that about.

- Make this week a celebration of your life by making a pilgrimage to a significant place for you. Plan a day to celebrate your life. Make up a litany of giving thanks for all you are grateful for.

- Put together an album of photos and mementos of joyous and wondrous times. Visit and talk with people from your past who gave you perspective on life.

- Celebrate your roots by attending an ethnic festival. Read poetry or prose from your heritage. Listen to its music.

- List the conflicts of your life that taught you something important. Conduct a dialogue with yourself about the conflicts that are most significant to you.

- Do something you've always wanted to do but never did because of fear. Give yourself a day of fun, a time of wonder and joy.

- Imagine how you can tell each person you love that you love them in a special way and start to do so. Be creative in how you do this.

Conclusion

The second half is a spiritual journey to explore your calling. Humbly seek help from others, your civic and sacred communities, your higher power. Seek spiritual companionship along the way. Don't try to go it alone as you did in the first half. Study the saints and sages of various faith traditions. Read spiritually uplifting books. They do not have to be overtly religious texts but those that bring you joy, peace, a sense of the sacred in the ordinary. Take an inventory of your life. Seek a spiritual guide whom you trust and admire. Develop a spiritual practice and follow it regularly, whether it be prayer, meditation, listening to music, or walking in nature. Let nature teach you and nourish you. Take time to reflect on the wonder and joy of your life. Develop an attitude of gratitude for all you have been given in life. Forgive yourself and others for things you have been holding onto too long. Maintain a personal journal of your spiritual experiences. Practice openness in all you do. Once in a while give in to an urge you would usually suppress. Try something odd or new. You just might learn something about who you are.

Chapter 11

How to Become a Wise Man

As you've seen, life's second half is no longer about power, possessions, and prestige. Also, you probably know more than you will ever need to know. You have more than you will ever need. Instead, the second half is about wisdom and rootedness. It is about letting go of the power you sought in life and finding a new form of power in being a wise man. As Winston Churchill once said, "We are all happier in many ways when we are old than when we are young. The young sow wild oats. The old grow sage."

The Source of Your Wisdom: Listening to Your Inner Voice

In life's first half you listened to the outer voices that told you what you needed to know. In the second half, you listen to your inner voices that tell you how to find a new source of wisdom.

Exercise: Attending to Your Inner Voice

1. Free yourself of the external voices that pressured you to achieve in the first half. Although you might not feel like you have accumulated enough at this point in life to feel secure, in all likelihood you have enough for the second half of life. Further pressuring yourself to achieve in the second half will be frustrating and difficult. Instead, focus your attention on the inner voices of each precious, passing day. Live in each present moment.

2. Recognize your inner voices that call you to interconnectedness with all. When you are in the present moment, you are free from the worries of the past or the future. It is time to fill your mind with tender moments and not regrets.

Start with a Beginner's Mind

An age-old technique in becoming wise is to take on what Buddhists call "the beginner's mind," to respond freshly to each moment as it arises, without prejudice and expectations. Beginner's mind is a state of openness and innocence that renders words and concepts obsolete. Jesus said that unless we come as a child (with a beginner's mind), we cannot enter the kingdom of heaven.

There are three phrases I have found helpful in developing a beginner's mind:

1. *"I don't know. What do you think?"* When you say this you find yourself comfortable in uncertainty, and there will be considerable uncertainty in the second half. It seems the more you feel you know, the less you really know. In the second half, you come to realize that much of life is a mystery, not to be solved (for perhaps there is no solution), but simply to sit with the questions. To be able to say "I don't know" frees you from the need to know everything, to have an answer for all questions, to be an expert. This requires that you separate yourself from the roles you once played. The good news is you don't need to be an expert anymore. It is quite acceptable to say, "I don't know."

2. *"That was good enough."* In the first half, it seemed that whatever you had was never enough. There was always more to

achieve, more to gain, more to earn. But freedom comes when you can put your head down on the pillow at night and say, "That was a good day. It was good enough," without any regrets, longing, or sense of things being incomplete. The key to being able to say "enough" is having an attitude of gratitude, being thankful for what you have, not longing for what you don't have. Can you say that whatever happened today was enough? Try saying that tomorrow and the next day.

3. *"I could be wrong."* This is perhaps the most freeing but most difficult of all the phrases you can have in the second half. In the first half, you want to be right in what you do or say. The second half means accepting that you don't have all the answers and what you think is right may not be. Are you willing to acknowledge that you could be wrong, that you don't know everything? If so, you are on your way to being a wise man.

Try saying each phrase three times daily and see how much freer you feel.

Extend and Seek Forgiveness

Jesus said in Luke 7:47, "the one to whom little is forgiven, loves little." Spiritual mentoring begins when you are able to let go of the anger, resentments, and hurts that you have been harboring for far too long. It is difficult to be wise when you are angry. Becoming wise requires that you repair the places of hurt—the broken promises, the acts of betrayal, the ruptures and heartaches that come with the territory of intimate relationships. All of us have unhealed, emotional scars that keep our hearts closed against repeated injury. The price you pay is that sections of your heart are locked shut, imprisoning both you and the people you have not forgiven. The energy you could be using to grow in wisdom is wasted on the brick and mortar of a hardened heart.

You may still be trying to teach someone a lesson that you think they deserve. You say, "How can I forgive him when he shows no regret and has not learned his lesson?" The emotional voucher you carry in your mind may never be paid off. It is you who ends up paying the price in wasted energy. Also, holding a grudge keeps you from gaining the wisdom of seeing your role in the wrongdoing. What anger and resentments are you holding that you need to let go of? How can you learn to forgive others?

It is also important for you to forgive yourself for your own wrongdoing. Part of becoming a wise man is to face your brokenness, the rejected inner self who sabotages you when you least expect it. In the 1970s there was a popular book entitled *I'm OK, You're OK*. But the fact is *you're not okay, and that's okay*. By facing your own need for forgiveness you see yourself as you are. Then, and only then, can you accept the grace that is offered to you in life and grow into being an elder. When you are able to know you are accepted just as you are, then you can change.

The outer appearance and reality reflects your inner being. Until you come to terms with your unrecognized shadow self, your efforts to practice forgiveness remain unfinished and your path toward becoming a wise man blocked.

It is important that you get past that which you continue to harbor in your heart and that which you need to makes amends for in your life. You will need to admit to yourself and to another human being the exact nature of your wrongs, to make a list of those harmed, and to make amends to them. These simple steps can assist you in clearing away your hurt and that which you have caused others. They can also lead you to greater wisdom.

Answer these questions in your journal:

⊠   What grudges do you still carry from the past? What reconciliation needs to be completed? Who do you need to forgive?

⊠   What do you need to forgive about yourself? What steps do you need to take to make amends for your wrongdoing? To whom? In what way?

⊠   Who should you tell about your wrongdoing?

Exercise: Seeking Forgiveness

Part 1: To assist you in the process of forgiveness, try the following exercise. Divide a piece of paper into three columns. In the first column, make a list of the people who have wronged you. In the second column, describe the apparent injustices that were inflicted on you. In the third column, explore how each has benefitted you in unforeseen ways. After each instance, repeat the following statement out loud, "I understand that you did me a great deal of good by your actions when you did _____ , for which I want to thank you. Now I forgive you and I am grateful for your contribution to my life."

Part 2: A second exercise is similar to the one in the chapter on fathers. Write a letter to someone or something that has hurt you, but don't send the letter to the offending party. Conclude the letter with the words "I completely release _____ from all my grudges of the past. We are both free to have a happier relationship now." An unsent letter is a wonderful expression of your deepest emotions and a tool for gaining closure and insight.

Part 3: A third exercise is to sit quietly and take a few deep breaths to center yourself. In your mind's eye, visualize being in the presence of someone toward whom you have unresolved issues, anger, or resentment. As you think about this person, consider how a lack of forgiveness drains energy and blocks your growth in wisdom. Place yourself in your adversary's shoes for a moment. What are their unacknowledged needs and wants? Move back and forth in your awareness between your issues and your adversary's. Give yourself an enlarged perspective and an objectivity to view the relationship anew. Imagine the two of you bathed in a ray of light that melts away your resentments and allows forgiveness by both parties. Rest in the warmth of this sunlight for a while. Now say, "I forgive you with all my heart and wish you nothing but goodness. I also forgive myself for my hardened heart. We will no longer suffer from this. I want both of us to be free to see the world with new eyes of wisdom." Feel the sense of weight being lifted from your life. Now, slowly open your eyes and relax a moment. When you return to the present moment, record your feelings and reactions in your journal.

These simple exercises can release you of the hurts you are harboring and create a new positive feeling that will propel you into the next step of becoming a wise man. Give yourself the gift of forgiveness today. It is the beginning of wisdom.

Learning to Live in a Youth-Oriented World

Unfortunately, in our society, the term "aging" connotes decline. Most men wince at the idea of going downward and inward in life's second half. Some say, "Is there another word for the journey, one that does not convey a sense of deterioration?" On the one hand men see aging as decline, a passive experience, something that happens *to* us. However, we fail to see the downward journey as an active process that turns the disadvantages of aging into something positive. We resist the latter because we associate it with the former; we don't initially understand that it promises transcendence. This is because we live in a youth-oriented culture. We praise youth in the media. We have exercise programs and cosmetics to keep us looking youthful. Try turning on the television and noticing how few roles are portrayed by people over sixty-five, how few commercials have older adults. When you notice how older people are depicted—silly, stubborn, vindictive, or, worst of all, cute—you begin to appreciate the not-so-subtle antipathy of a market-driven culture toward aging men and women. An older man is euphemistically described as "distinguished," but what is conveyed is "over-the-hill." A TV commercial says, "Look at the spots on my hand. They call these aging spots, but I call them ugly." What does this say about our attitudes toward the natural process of aging?

Getting older in a youth-oriented world becomes a necessary evil rather than an opportunity for spiritual transformation. Society would like to pretend that old men don't exist, except when we're frustrated with them for driving too slowly. For years, Theodore has looked at least ten years younger than he actually was. Now in his fifties with an eighteen-year-old daughter, Theodore is beginning to feel old. His baby face does not compensate for his gray hair and wrinkles. He said, "For the first time in my life, I feel like my age when I find myself with kids in their twenties, and they look at me like I am ancient. It is tough aging in a world that idealizes youth."

It is time that society overcomes these prejudices and demonstrates the value of aged wisdom. Perhaps the best image to overcome these prejudices is that of the wise, old, grandfatherly figures in our lives. If we recognized more of these men, perhaps society could overcome its bias against age, and men in the second half could better live in our youth-oriented culture. We can overcome this bias by recognizing the wisdom of aging men and transform the concept of aging into saging.

Grandfatherly Wisdom

Having had a child may be the only necessary precondition to becoming a grandparent. Yet, unlike each of the prior stages of fatherhood, becoming a grandfather is completely dependent on others. If my children remain childless, I do not become a grandfather to a blood relative. My children, as parents, will determine the frequency and the quality of grandfather-grandchild contact. In addition to proximity concerns, the parents' relationship with their own parents may dominate the children's experience of their grandparents. Today's society poses some difficulties for grandfathers: divorce of our children, geographic moves, and the breakup of the nuclear family. However, being a grandfather offers a man a special opportunity to be a mentor.

Grandfatherly figures, though, are not confined to those who actually grandparent a child. Some men display grandfatherly wisdom at an early age, such as Martin Luther King Jr., who died at thirty-nine. Mystic Thomas Merton and theologian Dietrich Bonhoeffer, two of the wisdom figures of the twentieth century, died young. So grandfatherliness connotes wisdom that is not simply attained in reaching a certain age. The qualities of grandfatherly wisdom are described in the next section.

Who are the grandfatherly figures you admire? Who would you like to emulate as you age? Perhaps the best way to describe a wise man is to name men you consider wise elders. List five men you see as sages, men with whom you would like to share qualities within yourself in the second half of your life.

What kind of elder do you want to be? How would you describe the wise man you wish to become? How would you like to be an elder to a child? Your sons and daughters and grandchildren? How would you like to be remembered by those who come after you? What would you like them to say about you? What role do you see yourself playing in educating boys about life and manhood? In what ways would you like to age? As your grandfathers did? How would you like to be different from your grandfathers?

Moving from Aging to Saging

Whether you ever become a grandfather, all men can become wise elders. In fact, no civilization has survived unless the elders have been willing to pass on their acquired wisdom to the young. First, an elder understands the five great spiritual truths of life:

1. **Life is hard.** In life there will be times of suffering, pain, loss, and hurt. As elders we accept the difficulties we will inevitably encounter in life.

2. **You are not in control.** In life's first half, you try to be in control, thinking you can manage whatever comes your way. However, in the second half, you see that you never were in control, despite your illusions that you were. Some of us learned this lesson through parenting. Whatever made us think we had control over our teenage children? Some of us learned this at the workplace as our organization changed despite our efforts to set its direction.

3. **You are going to die.** Although your birth certificate has no expiration date, we will all die at some time.

4. **You are not all that important.** Despite your attempts to live as if the world revolved around you, it doesn't. If you don't believe that, quit your job and see in five years if anyone remembers who you were.

5. **Your life is not about you.** There is a far greater story being told in life. You are an important part of that story, but there is something greater, cosmic, and sacred being played out. Your task is to find your part in the larger story being told.

Second, at its best, elder energy is quiet and secure, having been tested and not found wanting. As a sage, you do not need to prove yourself any longer, so you can approve the efforts of others more readily. Children feel secure in the presence of a sage because, while Mom and Dad are still rushing to find their way through life's journey, an elder can create space where the journey has found its purpose. A sage deeply trusts life precisely because he has come to terms with death. A sage knows that pain is not the enemy but that fear of pain is. A sage has lived through enough life to understand that, in the long run, life is stronger than death.

Third, a sage trusts life on its terms, stops trying to force life into little compartments, and allows it to flow in the patterns it chooses. This is not to say that an elder is passive. A sage has seen enough of death that he knows what it looks like, even when it comes under the guise of false promises and clever rationalizations. But he can look beyond the ignorance of the young who desire possessions, money, and power, with the wisdom of knowing that these are transitory illusions. He knows what is worth living for and what is not, what is worth seeking. Hopefully, by the time a man is in the second half, he knows what he seeks in his remaining years.

Fourth, a sage understands that every human decision inevitably mixes good and bad. Courage in the second half is not resisting pain and suffering or even death. Courage comes in affirming life. And life can be good. If you have walked the hero's journey in the first half, your beliefs now should have a radical openness to truth no matter what the consequences or where it leads.

Fifth, there is something both territorial and spacious about the wise man: he knows his boundaries as well as his center. He does not have to overprotect his boundaries or center. He shares his journey but does not force his experiences on anyone else.

Sixth, you become a wise man by learning to deal graciously with your limitations, which comes by facing concrete and frustrating limits. The joyful acceptance of a limited world is probably the clearest indication of mature, wise male energy.

Answer these questions in your journal:

☒ What are the spiritual truths that guide your life?

☒ Are you able to accept the good and bad of life with courage and strength?

☒ Have you accepted your limitations and do you joyfully accept a limited world?

Exercise: Life's Satisfactions

Find a comfortable space and a piece of paper. List in one column those things you consider to be bad in your life, the pain and suffering you have faced or now face. In another column list the good things, the joys and satisfactions of your life. Step back from the lists and see which is longer. Which list carries greater weight in your life? Now list the resources you have to stand in the middle of these polarities, holding them together in creative tension.

Humor: A Gift of a Wise Man

Humor is a hallmark of maturity, as Abraham Maslow, Carl Rogers, and many others have asserted. Humor is associated with empathy, self-confidence, and creativity. Freud said that humor is the highest and most mature mode of coping. As you mature, you are likely to rely more on humor. And the greater your psychological well-being, the greater your sense of humor (Chinen 1989). The mark of emotional health is to be able to cry from the heart and laugh from the belly.

Because men are usually more aggressive than women, we may have a greater need for humor. For men, humor is a tonic. Remember, a merry heart is good medicine. If you have ascended the ladder of success in the first half and now find yourself in a responsible position, humor is particularly important. When young men become frustrated, they rave about and rebel against the authority. But as a second-half man who has ascended the ladder, you have no such luxuries. You cannot fume about incompetent authorities, since, in many cases, you are the one in charge. American society does not like a whining middle-aged man. Nor can you simply leave the situation, as a youth might, because too many others, including your angry teens, depend on you for emotional and material security. Hemmed in by responsibilities, you might find yourself unable to fight or flee. Humor provides you a vital resource.

On the other hand, you may be in the second half and have never fully climbed the ladder of success. You may find yourself pushed off to the side. You may not call the shots and yet can still be taunted by youth with "Look at the mess you've left us. And you're a burden on us, besides!" Again, a sense of humor will make it easier to deal with where you find yourself at this stage of life. Humor in psychological healing helps mitigate stress and tragedy. Humor facilitates physical healing. Often, a good laugh may give you more relief from pain than narcotics.

Free Yourself to Play

Play, according to Webster's dictionary, is defined as "a brisk or free movement, amusement, free frolic." Play, as we age, really comes to be those activities that stand against your compulsion to do or produce, that which brings your being back to an appreciation for life in general. Play is your inner joy, outwardly expressed. It can be laughing, singing, dancing, swimming, cooking, running, or anything we have fun doing. Play makes all aspects of life more enjoyable. Play makes us feel younger and more positive.

You might not pursue play now; you are told "to act your age," whatever that means. You may have become concerned that people will think you are not mature. Play often happens in spite of you, such as when a bird calls you from your work by pecking at the window. Play happens when you go hiking with a friend and enjoy nature, or sit on the back porch reading a good book. All of these are forms of play. Some forms of play happen more so in life's second half as we are drawn to humor from a perspective of wisdom. Bonnie Raitt, the blues singer, says, "I have a sense of play and humor now that I did not have in my twenties or thirties, because it is born in wisdom" (2002).

It is the easy spirit that makes something playful. It is the capacity to enjoy the moment, without thinking, without being productive, and without long-range consequences. Real adult play has more to do with what you enjoy than what you think might be good for you. Free, nonproductive, enjoyable, renewing—these are the words that describe play. When you enjoy life, you begin to see the sacredness of all of life and live appreciatively.

When and how do you play? With whom do you feel comfortable to be yourself and act silly, playful, carefree? What gets in your way of being playful? It is time to grow up and play.

Generativity

As you age, you move into a time of harvesting the fruits of your lifetime's experience, enjoying them, and passing them on to younger people. When you harvest, you consciously celebrate the contributions you have made in your life. You appreciate the friendships you have nurtured, the people you can now mentor, and your wider involvement on behalf of the community, the nation, and the earth itself. It is a time of generativity, of experiencing from within quiet self-appreciation, honor, respect, and recognition from family, relatives, and colleagues. It is also a time to give back to others a portion of what you have so bounteously received in life.

Harvesting shows that you can still make a difference in the world. Your sense of meaning comes from being able to contribute to others. In the first half, you invested your time, energy, and aspirations in endeavors that you hoped would bear fruit in the symbols of success. In the second half, you may find that the impact was not what you thought it would be. Your work was not in vain, but not for the reasons you thought. Your relationships have borne fruit; your struggles have created meaning and value; your failures (of which there likely are many if you will admit it) unwittingly have led to a wisdom that is beyond any price.

Here are ways in which you can share your wisdom:

- Enjoy simple acts of living, acts of loving kindness.

- Be a storyteller who spins webs of enchanted, verbal magic that helps people understand their place in the cosmos.

- Become a master craftsman who may be less dependent upon sight and more open to vision, teaching younger people to be craftspersons, weaving them into the fabric of creation.

- Become a prankster who teaches young people that life should be fun as well as having a few serious moments.

- Become an elder who settles disputes, a person who may speak softly and rarely at social meetings, but when they speak, people listen.

- Become a sacred ecologist who preserves the world's beauty and harmony. Become a mobilizer of social change.

- Be a beloved pathfinder, beckoning others to enter the province of aging in anticipation of growing in strength and usefulness to society.

When you do these things, your graying hair becomes a crown of glory and your wrinkles a mark of distinction of a wise man. As you age with grace, younger people will be exposed to images of elders that highlight inner beauty and radiance. Others will view your aging as the summit of life, not the end of it.

Generativity requires that you work within the evolution of life, in touch with the traditions of the past, and that you transmit the living flame of wisdom to help the young meet their own challenges. In your younger years, to pursue your dreams of success, you used a close-up lens. This way you could concentrate on what was immediately before you. Now, in the second half you are like a camera with a wide-angle lens that can encompass both the timeless ground that supports life and the ever-changing figure in the foreground that compels your momentary interests. You feel connected to the world through bonds of empathy. Life hopefully has become more poetic, and you see yourself surrounded by trees, clouds, and animals shimmering with metaphoric insight, revealing depths of meaning that eluded your youthful mind.

To be a generative wise man, you welcome back your capacity for feeling and intuition that you sacrificed in your pursuit of success. It is to be at ease with tender feelings, responding to beauty and the suffering of others with a deepened sense of empathy. Besides enjoying a friendlier relationship with your softer side, you also have the ability to speak with authority and wisdom.

Philosopher Martin Buber says the aging male helps forge a center in the younger person. You do not impose doctrines on others in an attempt to clone yourself. Rather, you evoke the individuality of others, applauding them as they struggle to clarify their values and discover their authentic path. A wise man allows the young to talk about their failures and shortcomings, their indiscretions and foibles, without feeling judged or shamed. He allows the young to feel respected and appreciated, in large part because he does not treat the young as underlings. Instead, through compassionate ways, a natural unfolding takes place that signals when the accumulated wisdom of a lifetime reaches the state of overflowing. This form of saging preserves valuable life experience from disappearing with the inevitable decay of the body.

As a wise man you leave a legacy in the wisdom that you have synthesized through decades of difficult learning. What you have to teach is not only verbal information and your technical skills, for these can be acquired in books. You impart wisdom from personal attitudes, moral and ethical judgments, and aesthetic appreciation, fired by a unique experience and the give-and-take of a living dialogue with an apprentice. True wise men are not in a hurry to impose their knowledge on others. The best sage gives an ear to others, lets them try out new ideas, and listens attentively and non-judgmentally without forming premature conclusions and short-circuiting youthful initiative and enthusiasm. In fact, sometimes the greatest transmission occurs from wordless, attentive listening.

A generative wise man is a "permissionary," giving others permission to carry on the work of self-exploration. He deepens their ability to keep the questions alive while he journeys himself. Although the traditional saying is that when the student is ready, the teacher will appear, the converse is also true. When the mentor is ready, the pupil will appear. Your change of being provides all the preparation needed for the students to present themselves.

The following are guidelines for beginning to be a wise man. With great spaciousness of heart and mind, listen to the other's genuine concerns before attempting to share your wisdom. Don't impose your knowledge, but evoke the other's innate knowing. Don't try to impress the other by claiming to be perfect, all knowing. Respect and call forth the other's uniqueness. Recognize that, like everything else, being a wise man has its seasons. There is a time to gain, a time to sow, as the book of Ecclesiastes reminds us. Realize you have a greater capacity than the young do to see life and its connectedness. This wisdom comes less from books than from the kitchen table, from work, from the playground, and from sacred moments when you are aware of the presence of something greater than yourself. Evoke the potential in others by widening their vision of human unfoldment. Contribute wisdom, balanced judgment, and enduring values to society. Offer examples of how to overcome limiting beliefs that fill people with needless negativity.

Answer these questions in your journal:

☒ What does generativity mean to you? What do you want to pass on to others?

☒ In what ways can you become a sage in life?

☒ How ready are you now to pass on your wisdom and experience to others?

The desire to manage the changes in your life is your greatest obstacle to wisdom. You must be open to all that change contains, including that which seems most threatening. How do you do that?

• Learn to lose track of time through a present focus. When you are in the present moment, it is the eternal present. Begin to discover hidden dimensions to everyday experiences that have always been there for you, but were veiled by time.

- Realize that this moment is a doorway into eternity. It means paying attention to the sacredness of everyday life, not viewing time as something to be spent or wasted, nor something you have or don't have. Time is sacred, a spiritual gift. Let go of what is weighing down your appreciation of the present moment.

Exercise: Leaving a Legacy Behind

Answer these questions in your journal:

1. Who are the people in your life that you would like to leave a legacy with, in terms of not monetary rewards but your spiritual strength? List these people on a piece of paper.

2. List what you would like to teach each person from your experience. What you have to teach may be different for each individual. What would you offer each one?

3. Now write three steps you can take today to begin to be a mentor to each person. Be specific in what you will do to become a wise sage to a younger person.

Learn the Tales of the Clan

One of the tasks of aging is telling the tales of the clan. In primitive cultures the task of elders was to tell the foundational stories of the tribe: where it came from and where it was going. They told tales of primal identity and vocation. They told the old tales of the nation, religion, or family roots. Passing on the wisdom of the clan is a vital task of creative aging. You are now an elder. Telling stories of your tradition can provide a desperately needed prophetic imagination to the cultural scene. Invite yourself to rediscover stories with power to reveal truth and falsehood, good and evil. Offer the power to transform yourself and the world.

The telling of tales lays the groundwork and prepares the soil for the next season and next generation. What tales of your clan would you pass on to the next generation? What wisdom of your family is vital for you to share with others? What stories and traditions do you want to pass on to youth? You will find it amazing, despite your thoughts that no one really wants to listen to your stories of old, that many young people crave to hear your stories. There is such richness in your past. Tell the story. Pass on to others the tales of your clan.

Also, find your elders and listen to their stories. Tape-record their experiences in the great stock market crash of 1929, the Depression years, World War II, the fifties. If you are blessed to know people who lived through World War I, ask them to tell you about that time. Sometimes having old photos around will help trigger their recollection. You will be greatly enriched by listening to the tales of your elders.

A Call to Action

It has been said that a prophet is a mystic in action. Becoming a wise man requires not only that you be a wise sage, but also that you act on behalf of the well-being of others and the earth. Contemplation without action is too inwardly focused. Action without wisdom and contemplation is shallow. Both are required. This means that in aging, you need to be clear what is in the best interest of others and the earth, to stand for justice and truth, to become a peacemaker on behalf of the world. There are several examples of such wise older men. One is former President Jimmy Carter, who may have had more impact on the world as an ex-president than as president of the United States. He has served as a peacemaker around the world. Mahatma Gandhi stood for peace and justice in the world until the very end of his life. Nelson Mandela has had a great impact on the world, perhaps more so as an elder statesman than in his youth. Desmond Tutu, an advocate for peace and justice, has had increased respect and influence in his latter years. Others in my life who thought globally and acted locally are Mark Lancaster, a social worker who worked for years with the Heifer Project in Maryland, providing funds to give cows, sheep, and goats to poor farmers to feed their families. Stephen Brown and Rick Rush from my church gave their time on weekends to assist Habitat for Humanity in building low-cost homes for those unable to afford a house. Others stood in lines demonstrating against war and oppression. Some served simple meals at local soup kitchens. Who are the men whom you respect who have shown wisdom and stood up for justice and action against oppression?

If you are a baby boomer, in your youth you likely were galvanized one way or another around the issues related to the Vietnam War, the environment, peace and justice, women's rights, civil rights, hunger in the world, and so forth. But over time you likely have lost some of that fire amidst the responsibilities of raising a family, working, and being a good provider. What part of the old calling to peace and justice issues, civil rights, and other action still burns within you? How much of that passion is waiting to be born anew, with the wisdom and maturity brought by age in contrast to the white-hot fire of your youth?

The beginning of wisdom and the call to action starts in a spirit of compassion for others. Compassion is not about feeling sorry for another person, but about being with them in their pain and suffering, often in silent presence. The Hebrew Scriptures give a wonderful example of holding together the tension of opposites—action and contemplation, compassion and justice—in Psalms 85:4: "Righteousness and peace have met together, mercy and truth have kissed each other." As a sage you are called to hold together in creative tension the polarity of opposites: mercy and truth, compassion and knowledge, righteousness and peace.

This is a time of life for you to utilize the wealth of your wisdom, to impact on the world. It may take the form of being involved in your local community to provide a safe haven for youth, promoting an anti–drug abuse effort in your town, working to clean up the environment, or standing against homelessness, violence, and hunger in your city, the nation, the world. It matters little how big or small your action may be. You need not impact the world—just your corner of it. Get involved! Don't sit on the sidelines. Act now! Join together your wisdom and your passion to make an impact on the world in which you live.

Answer these questions in your journal:

☒ What dreams have you left behind as you sought to climb the ladder of success? What dreams remain burning within you that yearn to be lived?

☒ How do you want to be involved in the struggles for peace and justice in the world? How could you impact these issues at a local as well as global level?

Learning to Love Anew

In life's second half, you need to find new values for living. This means moving from competing to connecting. Developing new values requires learning to love differently than in life's first half, for it involves being open to both giving and receiving—from the heart and not just from the head or wallet. To love again differently means being willing to simply listen to others, to empathize and not always try to fix what may be wrong, to hear the feelings expressed. Loving anew requires being able to show a friend how much you care for him and being able to accept affection. It means connecting to nature and the spiritual dimension. Essential to becoming a wise man is to learn anew, or perhaps for the first time, how to truly love.

How can you maintain a loving heart in the presence of evil, violence, and hatred in the world? This is a big question. Make no mistake about it, evil does exist in the world. If you doubt that, simply turn on the evening news and listen to stories of genocide, other atrocities, wars, starvation of innocent children, and even internal conflicts that bring people to do desperate things. Being able to face such evil with a loving heart requires new eyes that seek not retribution but justice and mercy. Such new love cannot just come from within yourself. It requires the indwelling of life that brings us to an awareness of a far greater story being played out in life. Faith enables us to find meaning in tragedy, hope in despair, and love amidst hatred.

This eternal love should be that which draws you in life. How open are you to the love that has existed in the world since the beginning of time? To start, you must remind yourself of what or whom you have loved before and love now. This requires finding what gives you great joy and peace in your life. This is your journey to the core of what you were made to be and the discovery of a peace that passes all understanding.

One of my most powerful experiences of love was at Mother Teresa's home for orphans and dying children in Haiti. I held dying children, frolicked on the swing set with those well enough to go to the playground, and prayed for mercy over infants as they struggled with the pain of malaria, malnutrition, AIDS, TB, and so many other illnesses. In the faces of Mother Teresa's sisters there was a radiant love. Amidst dire situations and death everywhere, the sisters acted only with love for these children. In the faces of the infants, they saw the face of the sacred. Their prayer every morning spoke to the source of this love:

> *Shine through us, that every soul we come in contact with*
> *may feel Your Presence in us. Stay with us so we may serve*
> *as You shine. May none of it be ours, but You. May we preach*
> *without preaching, not by words but by example. By the*
> *catching force, the sympathetic influence of what we do, the*
> *evident fullness of the love our hearts bear to You. May it be*
> *so for us today.*

Now, we are not all saints like these sisters, but that same love can shine in our lives, in and through us. This is the love that can develop with age, which can radiate most brightly when we let go of the needs of the past and rest in the assurances of love and peace given to us.

Answer these questions in your journal:

- ☒ How do you experience love in your daily life? What is required for you to cultivate love anew for yourself, others, and the world?

- ☒ What changes are you willing to make in your life to experience that love and to convey that love to others? What disciplines or sources of inspiration might assist you in manifesting more love in the world?

- ☒ What would it mean for you to put love into action more so in your life?

Conclusion

Becoming a wise man is the fruit of living. Wisdom harvests and integrates the joys, sorrows, glories, mediocrity, and even evil of a lifetime. It transfigures everything. It goes before and behind you, breaking through and consuming into life the dyings of a lifetime.

The spiraling path toward being a wise man is largely unmarked and not easy to follow. It confronts you with unfamiliar passages to be mastered. But aging men can discover the path to being a wise man and branch out to open up alternate routes. Aging is not just about increasing your longevity. We have added years to our life. It is time that we add abundant life to those years. Simply increasing your years left to live does not promise you a rich and wise second half of life. Aging well requires you to become a wise man, a sage, who draws on a new set of values, a deeper understanding of yourself, a greater appreciation of your innate and acquired wisdom, and a deeper capacity to love. These are the building blocks to becoming a wise man.

Conclusion

This book has given a road map for playing life's second half. On this road map we have explored some of the side roads we know of along the way. You will face many other side roads that you cannot foresee at this time. The exciting part of playing life's second half is that the game plans you had going into the first half of life are likely no longer useful. You need to throw out the old, unhelpful playbook. The reality is, there is no playbook for life's second half, only somewhat vague road maps or plans that can point you in a certain direction. Until you play life's second-half game, until you travel down the second-half road, you will not know where you are going. You will only be able to see where you have been. The essence of this journey is that you have to play the game in your own, unique way.

Focus now on where you really want to be when the game is over. What gives you life, passion, love, satisfaction, and most importantly, significance? From here on, regardless of what plans you make or roads you take, choose the road *you* want to take; and if it brings life, love, and health, if it brings you closer to your true self, it will be a meaningful journey for you. Remember, playing life's second half in your own way—not the end goal, not the destination—is what matters.

Rainer Maria Rilke, the Austrian poet, reminds us that our life is not a steeply sloping hill as in the first half of life, where we hurry to see the top so we can better see what is behind us. In the second half, we are often in the beautiful dales and valleys between hills or maybe even on the downside of the hill. Rilke says life is often like the rest between notes, which may at times feel like being in a desert, in discord. In the second half, more often than not, you will find yourself in this wonderful, lush valley where you need to harvest the fruit you had sown in life's first half, but it will mean holding together the tension of opposites. In the interval between life and death, you find that the mountains continue to form, the hills refresh themselves with new life, and the song of renewal and hope flows on and on.

Resources

For Work

Workaholics Anonymous
World Services Organization
P.O. Box 289
Menlo Park, CA 94026
(510) 273-9253
http://people.ne.mediaone.net/wa2

On Parenting

Dads and Daughters, Inc.
P.O. Box 3458
Duluth, MN 55803
(888) 824-3247
www.dadsanddaughters.org

On Aging

Administration on Aging
330 Independence Avenue, SW

Washington, DC 20201
(800) 677-1116
www.aoa.dhhs.gov/aoa/webres/craig.htm

Generations United
440 First Street, NW, Suite 310
Washington, DC 20001
(202) 662-4283
www.gu.org/gul.html

Information on Aging
U.S. Bureau of Commerce
U.S. Census Bureau
Washington, DC 20233
(301) 457-4100
www.census.gov/population/www/socdemo/age.html

Additional Resources

Ackerman, Robert. 1994. *Silent Sons: A Book for and about Men.* New York: Firestone Books.

Andronico, Michael P. (ed.). 1996. *Men in Groups: Insights, Interventions, and Psychoeducational Work.* Washington, DC: American Psychological Association.

Biddulph, Steve. 1995. *Manhood: An Action Plan for Changing Men's Lives.* Sydney, Australia: Finch Publishing.

Bolen, Jean Shinoda. 1989. *Gods in Everyman: A New Psychology of Men's Lives and Loves.* New York: Harper Personal.

Brewi, Janice, and Anne Brennan. 1988. *Mid-Life Spirituality and Jungian Archetypes.* York Beach, Maine: Nicolas-Hays.

Bridges, William. 1991. *Managing Transitions: Making the Most of Change.* Cambridge, Mass.: Perseus Publishing.

Boyd, Stephen B. 1995. *The Men We Long to Be: Beyond Domination to a New Christian Understanding of Manhood.* San Francisco: Harper San Francisco.

Cohen, Gene D. 2000. *The Creative Age: Awakening Human Potential in the Second Half of Life.* New York: Quill.

Cooper, Mark D., and Rose Brunette Dean. 1997. *Get a Life: A Second Chance after 50.* Great Falls, Virg.: Information International.

Farrell, Warren. 1993. *The Myth of Male Power*. New York: Simon and Schuster.

Garbarino, James. 1999. *Lost Boys: Why Our Sons Turn Violent and How We Can Save Them*. New York: Anchor Books.

Gerzon, Mark. 1982. *A Choice of Heroes: The Changing Face of American Manhood*. Bridgewater, N.J.: Replica Books.

Gerzon, Mark. 1992. *Listening to Midlife: Turning Your Crisis into a Quest*. Boston: Shambhala.

Groff, Kent I. 1999. *Journeymen: A Spiritual Guide for Men (and Women Who Want to Understand Them)*. Nashville: Upper Room Books.

Guenther, Margaret. 1995. *Toward Holy Ground: Spiritual Directions for the Second Half of Life*. Boston: Cowley Publications.

Johnson, Robert A. 1991. *Transformation: Understanding the Three Levels of Masculine Consciousness*. San Francisco: Harper San Francisco.

Keen, Sam. 1991. *Fire in the Belly: On Being a Man*. New York: Bantam Books.

Kipnis, Aaron R. 1991. *Knights without Armor: A Practical Guide for Men in Quest of Masculine Soul*. Los Angeles: J. P. Tarcher, Inc.

Kotre, John N., and Elizabeth Hall. 1997. *Seasons of Life: The Dramatic Journey from Birth to Death*. Ann Arbor: University of Michigan Press.

Lakritz, Kenneth R., and Thomas M. Knoblauch. 1999. *Elders on Love: Dialogues on the Consciousness, Cultivation, and Expression of Love*. New York: Parabola Books.

Lazear, Jonathon. 2001. *The Man Who Mistook His Job for a Life: A Chronic Overachiever Finds the Way Home*. New York: Crown Publishers.

Levinson, Daniel J. 1978. *The Seasons of a Man's Life*. New York: Ballantine Books. New York: Fawcett Columbine.

Nerburn, Kent. 1993. *Letters to My Son: Reflections on Becoming a Man*. San Rafael, Calif.: New World Library.

Osherson, Samuel. 1992. *Wrestling with Love: How Men Struggle with Intimacy with Women, Children, Parents, and Each Other*. New York: Fawcett Columbine.

Osherson, Samuel, and Stephan B. Poulter. 1986. *Finding Our Fathers: How a Man's Life Is Shaped by His Relationship with His Father*.

Pasick, Robert. 1992. Awakening from the Deep Sleep: A Powerful Guide for Courageous Men. San Francisco: Harper San Francisco.

Pasick, Robert. 1992. *Awakening from the Deep Sleep: A Powerful Guide for Courageous Men.* San Francisco: Haper San Francisco.

Peterson, Peter G. 1999. *Gray Dawn: How the Coming Age Wave Will Transform America—and the World.* New York: Random House.

Raines, Howell. 1993. *Fly Fishing through the Midlife Crisis.* New York: Anchor Books.

Raines, Robert. 1997. *A Time to Live: Seven Steps of Creative Aging.* New York: Plume Books.

Rohr, Richard. 1999. *Everything Belongs: The Gift of Contemplative Prayer.* New York: Crossroads Publishing Company.

Zinn, Jack. 2002. *Older Men's Business: Valuing Relationships, Living with Change.* Sydney, Australia: Finch Publishing.

References

Albom, Mitch. 1997. *Tuesdays with Morrie: An Old Man, a Young Man, and Life's Greatest Lessons.* Grand Haven, Mich.: Brilliance.

Ayto, John. 1990. *Dictionary of Word Origins.* New York: Arcade Publishing.

Berry, Wendell. 1985. *Collected Poems: 1957-1982.* New York: Farrar, Straus, and Giroux.

Bonhoeffer, Dietrich. 1954. *Life Together: The Classic Exploration of Faith in Community.* London: SCM Press.

Campbell, Joseph, and Bill Moyers. 1988. *The Power of Myth.* New York: Doubleday.

Carter, Jimmy. 1998. *The Virtues of Aging.* New York: Ballantine Books.

Chinen, Allan B. 1989. *In the Ever After: Fairy Tales and the Second Half of Life.* Wilmette, Ill.: Chiron Publications.

Dalai Lama. 1996. *The Good Heart: A Buddist Perspective on The Teachings of Jesus.* Boston: Wisdom Publications.

Dass, Ram, Mark Matousek, and Marlene Roeder. 2000. *Still Here: Embracing Aging, Changing, and Dying.* New York: Riverhead Books.

Dychtwald, Ken. 1999. *Age Power: How the 21st Century Will Be Ruled by the New Old.* New York: Putnam.

Eckhart, Meister. 1996. *Meister Eckhart from Whom God Hid Nothing.* Boston: Shambhala.

Erikson, Erik H., Joan M. Erikson, and Helen Q. Kivnick. 1986. *Vital Involvement in Old Age.* New York: Norton.

Hardin, Paula Payne. 1992. *What Are You Doing with the Rest of Your Life? Choices in Midlife.* Novato, Calif.: New World Library.

Hesse, Hermann. 1951. *Siddhartha.* New York: Bantam.

Hillman, James. 1993. *The Soul's Code: In Search of Calling and Character.* New York: Harper.

Holy Bible, The. 1990. New Revised Standard Version. Nashville: Thomas Nelson.

Jung, Carl. 1972. *Selected Letters of C. G. Jung, 1909-1961.* Edited by Gerhard Adler. Princeton, N.J.: Princeton University Press.

Jung, Carl, Emma Jung, and Toni Wolff. 1982. *Letters.* San Francisco: The Analytic Psychology Club of San Francisco.

Kelly, Thomas R. 1992. *A Testament of Devotion.* San Francisco: Harper San Francisco.

Merton, Thomas. 1956. *Thoughts in Solitude.* New York: Farrar, Straus, and Giroux.

Moyers, Bill. 1989. Interview with Bill Moyers. *Esquire,* July, 145.

O'Donohue, John. 1997. *Anam Cara: A Book of Celtic Wisdom.* New York: Cliff Street Books.

Peters, Thomas J., and Robert H. Waterman Jr. 1988. *In Search of Excellence: Lessons from America's Best-Run Companies.* New York: Warner Books.

Raitt, Bonnie. 2002. Interview on National Public Radio. October 28.

Rilke, Rainer Maria. 1996. *Rilke's Book of Hours: Love Poems to God.* New York: Riverhead Books.

Rilke, Rainer Maria. 1981. *Selected Poems of Rainer Maria Rilke.* New York: Harper and Row.

Rinpoche, Sogyal.1993. *The Tibetan Book of Living and Dying.* Edited by Patrick D. Gaffney and Andrew Harvey. San Francisco: Harper San Francisco.

Schachter-Shalomi, Zalman, and Ronald S. Miller. 1995. *From Age-ing to Sage-ing: A Profound New Vision of Growing Older.* New York: Warner Books.

Semple, Ellen Churchill. 1911. *Influences of Geographic Environment.* New York: Henry Holt and Co.

Shapiro, Jerrold Lee. 1993. *The Measure of a Man: Becoming the Father You Wish Your Father Had Been.* New York: Delacorte Press.

Sheehy, Gail. 1998. *Understanding Men's Passages: Discovering the New Map of Men's Lives.* New York: Ballantine Books.

Smith, Huston. 2001. *Why Religion Matters: The Fate of the Human Spirit in an Age of Disbelief.* San Francisco: Harper San Francisco.

St. John of the Cross. 1995. *The Dark Night of the Soul.* New York: Fount.

Teilhard de Chardin, Pierre. 1968. *Letters to Two Friends, 1926-1952.* New York: New American Library.

Tillich, Paul. 1951. *Systematic Theology.* Vol. 1. Chicago: University of Chicago Press.

Vaillant, George E. 2002. *Aging Well: Surprising Guideposts to a Happier Life from the Landmark Harvard Study of Adult Development.* Boston: Little, Brown and Company.

Ventura, Michael. 1990. The solution to all our problems (guaranteed). *The Utne Reader,* July/August, 145.

Whyte, David. 1994. *Heart Aroused: Poetry and the Preservation of the Soul of Corporate America.* New York: Currency Paperback.

Some Other New Harbinger Titles

Helping Your Depressed Child, Item 3228 $14.95

The Couples's Guide to Love and Money, Item 3112 $18.95

50 Wonderful Ways to be a Single-Parent Family, Item 3082 $12.95

Caring for Your Grieving Child, Item 3066 $14.95

Helping Your Child Overcome an Eating Disorder, Item 3104 $16.95

Helping Your Angry Child, Item 3120 $17.95

The Stepparent's Survival Guide, Item 3058 $17.95

Drugs and Your Kid, Item 3015 $15.95

The Daughter-In-Law's Survival Guide, Item 2817 $12.95

Whose Life Is It Anyway?, Item 2892 $14.95

It Happened to Me, Item 2795 $17.95

Act it Out, Item 2906 $19.95

Parenting Your Older Adopted Child, Item 2841 $16.95

Boy Talk, Item 271X $14.95

Talking to Alzheimer's, Item 2701 $12.95

Helping a Child with Nonverbal Learning Disorder or Asperger's Syndrome, Item 2779 $14.95

The 50 Best Ways to Simplify Your Life, Item 2558 $11.95

When Anger Hurts Your Relationship, Item 2604 $13.95

The Couple's Survival Workbook, Item 254X $18.95

Loving Your Teenage Daughter, Item 2620 $14.95

The Hidden Feeling of Motherhood, Item 2485 $14.95

Parenting Well When You're Depressed, Item 2515 $17.95

Thinking Pregnant, Item 2302 $13.95

Call **toll free, 1-800-748-6273,** or log on to our online bookstore at **www.newharbinger.com** to order. Have your Visa or Mastercard number ready. Or send a check for the titles you want to New Harbinger Publications, Inc., 5674 Shattuck Ave., Oakland, CA 94609. Include $4.50 for the first book and 75¢ for each additional book, to cover shipping and handling. (California residents please include appropriate sales tax.) Allow two to five weeks for delivery.

Prices subject to change without notice.